MW01278440

On Fire

A Memoir

By Steph West

Red Fern Press

Red Fern Press books may be purchased for educational, business, or sales promotional use. For more information, please e-mail the marketing department at redfernpressquery@gmail.com.

Second Edition

Cover design, Anna Conley // Photography, Aaron Massey

ISBN 979-8-9887672-1-3 (Kindle)
ISBN 979-8-9887672-0-6 (Paperback)
ISBN 979-8-9887672-2-0 (Hardback)

For my daughter, whose wide-open heart and endless belief in every good thing helps me stay the course.

And for all the women still fighting for their right to be heard, have choices, and stay alive.

Acknowledgements

Thank you to author Rebecca Solnit for use of the epigraph from *Men Explain Things to Me* (Haymarket Books) copyright Rebecca Solnit 2014 reprinted here with the author's permission.

Thank you to my editor, Andra Paitz, to whom I am eternally grateful for the patience, the wisdom, and the great conversations. Editors are the lifeblood of writers. Thank you for seeing that which is unseen by the narrator. To my daughter, for letting me tell our story and being the best part of it. To my mother and brother, two of the three musketeers. We were always rich in the things that mattered even when we were poor. To my stepfather, for being present when you didn't have to be and for showing us the world as it could be not as it was. To Ms. Gamer, for sticking around through the worst of it and then reading and reading and reading some more. To Ms. Navarre, for bringing me the essentials and hope when there was little of them. To Ms. Elementary, for many days and nights of babysitting so I could work, and for being so kind when you did. To the two Upper Arlington mothers (and your beautiful families), who saved our lives. To all the early readers of my fiction and nonfiction, thank you. Your feedback was, and is, invaluable. And to Mr. Politico, for always being there and never getting the proper credit until now.

Author's Note About the Truth

This book is a work of creative nonfiction. Like any collection of memories, written or recalled, it is likely to contain inconsistencies, contradictions, or outright errors. Names have been changed, some timelines compressed, and some composites of characters created for both brevity and to protect the individual and their version of events. Keep in mind, as with any memoir, this is my truth as I see it. And every version of any truth has its equal and opposite counterpart.

For my family and friends: relationships are complicated. My door is always open.

On Fire

A Memoir

Table of Contents

Content Warnings

Some chapters in this book contain stories of childhood sexual abuse and adult sexual assault. It could be triggering for survivors. If you need support, you can call the National Sexual Assault Hotline 24/7 at (800) 656-HOPE (4673). To report a crime, please call 911 or go to your nearest law enforcement agency. For more information, visit rainn.org/resources.

Some chapters in this book contain stories of attempted suicide, suicidal ideation, and anxiety and panic disorder incidents experienced by adults and minors. If you or your child is in crisis, the National Suicide Prevention Lifeline is now the 988 Suicide and Crisis Lifeline. Just text or call 988, and you will be immediately connected to a mental health professional. You can also chat with a professional at 988lifeline.org/chat. Veterans can call 988 and press one. An additional tool for parents and minors dealing with mental health issues is On Our Sleeves from Nationwide Children's Hospital in Columbus, Ohio. Visit onoursleeves.org for more information.

Please note, my viewpoints on psychoactive medication are my own. Medication is a valuable and necessary tool in the treatment of mental health issues for most people.

Epigraph

"Most women fight wars on two fronts, one for whatever the putative topic is and one simply for the right to speak, to have ideas, to be acknowledged to be in possession of facts and truths, to have value, to be a human being. Things have gotten better, but this war won't end in my lifetime. I'm still fighting it, for myself certainly, but also for all those younger women who have something to say, in the hope that they will get to say it."

~ **Rebecca Solnit,** *Men Explain Things to Me*

Prologue

Dear Mama,

You should know, I'm worried about me, too.

I've made myself a reputation of being able to get out of anything, fix everything that's broken, find paths that don't exist or, when necessary, create them myself. It's the hallmark of who I am and the one characteristic that has sustained me. I may have started my life malleable, but now I've hardened into steel to become the tough and unyielding foundation of my and Savannah's lives.

She was born into this life as flint: durable, beautiful, capable of weathering any storm, and sparking me to life. But now, our lives are like kindling soaked in kerosene. And with one smack of flint to steel, it will all burn down around us.

In the darkness of my room with the cool fan blowing on my hot face, I wonder if you ever felt this way while you were raising Brother and me. I remember the cramped room you and I shared after your divorce. There wasn't enough money for three bedrooms, so you and I had white, twin beds in the big room while Brother had his own room right next to us.

I don't know what you were feeling, but perhaps now I can guess as I share a small basement with Savannah in someone else's house. Our home is long gone. She and I sometimes catch a glimpse of each other during the night across the few inches of

1

space that exist between us, and I always smile even when I can feel the tears mounting. She can't see me cry even though in this one painful moment we are penniless and lost. She can only know that I will turn it right side up. I promised her, and I cannot—must not—break that promise without unraveling all the strength it took to get here.

It must not have been easy for you to leave, given how hard it is for women even now. When I left, despite the improved laws and the women's movements, I still got the looks, the disapproval, the ostracism—much more than Mr. Husband. So, it must have been downright scandalous when you took off and created a new life for the three of us. To tell them all to go to hell and do what was best for you. You were the original rebel.

I believe you did the right thing. It wasn't popular, but I don't care what anyone else thought. I'm guessing you cried, but I never saw it if you did. I only cared that we were together, the three musketeers. And having my mother as my roommate at ten years old was better than all the crystallized sugar at the penny candy store. It was a constant comfort to know I could glance across the cramped room and see you there. The rhythmic way you breathed allowed me to fall asleep even amid our extraordinary trials.

On the day I was born, it was just you and me then too. You were alone, in the hospital, on that military base, in your twenties, with family miles

2

away, giving birth next to a nurse who kept screaming at you to just "Push!"

That was year one.

Throughout my childhood at night after dinner, I would wiggle in my seat at the kitchen table as I impatiently waited for you to pull out your drawing pad. It was filled with the most fantastic characters I'd ever seen: beautiful princesses and one very lovely drawing of Bambi, a favorite. I'd sit and watch your fingers carefully guide the pencil from line to line as an image appeared, as if by magic, under the spell of your number two wand.

When bedtime rolled around, you would read to me. Calm and peaceful, funny and loud, or dark and scary, depending on what the text called for. You were so tired, but you did it anyway even though you had to get up early the next day and go back to work in sterile supply at the local hospital.

At the time, I didn't understand why drawing wasn't your job. I understand now.

I'm sure you felt the push and pull of your reality, knowing you were talented but seeing the life in front of you and being responsible for it. The balancing act of dreams and reality, magic and ordinary. You always leaned toward the hard truths of life as the steering wheel of your purpose and meaning. You had to. I wish it would have been different for you. Even now, I can feel a surge of disappointment in the people who should have been

3

paying attention to you and guiding you. But because of life's realities, they simply could not.

Who would you have been if you had been encouraged to go to art school? If someone had pulled you aside and said, "My goodness, you're talented." If your twenties had been spent painting with bright reds, blues, and greens on canvases instead of painting your face in front of a mirror wishing for a different life. What if someone had encouraged your talent? Celebrated it, even. Helped you understand that what you did as an artist was pure enchantment.

I may not have existed, I realize. Had you gone to art school, I never would have been born because you would have captured someone's eye, I have no doubt. You would have learned, worked hard, and found some clever job creating beautiful pieces for someone. Your confidence would have grown, and your eyes would have been focused on the drawing in front of you, the world in front of you, and how you could shape it with just a little bit of magic.

Instead, you married and raised a family. It was a noble calling of course but a stark contradiction to your talents and in a time when you had to choose one or the other, when being both a mother and something else was only just coming into fashion. You didn't deserve the way you were treated during this time of your life. Brother saw more than I did, but I knew things weren't right. I don't know what

4

caused a shift in you, but I'm glad that at some point you realized you were worth more. That Brother and I deserved more.

The three of us piled into your tan Volkswagen bug, which had been packed to the brim, and I watched from the backseat as everything from my childhood disappeared into a hazy blur. I never minded the government-subsidized housing complex we lived in after that. You may have felt bad about it. I know you were concerned about money, how angry Brother was, studying for your next LPN exam, and trying to figure out how you were going to get through each day, but we were okay. We had each other, sometimes we had meat for taco salad, and every now and again we got cassette tapes when your paycheck had a little bit more. That was enough.

You walking out the door cracked open the door of possibility for us.

You made a choice, for better or worse, to stand up for yourself. To at least, by God, *try* to become something better than the life you were living. Your irreverence and defiance toward the lingering notion of 1950s homemaking and sexual politics made every lonely night in our post-divorce world worth the price of admission. I admired your rebellion, then bore it out in my bones.

I see now, as a mother, that I could not have been an easy child. You once said that maybe you didn't know how to raise me. That I was hard to parent. I learned too fast, moved too quickly, sunk

5

into myself, and spoke very little. I was captivated by the words and all the stories inside beautifully bound leather books and heavily worn paperbacks. I was in love with a world you didn't understand, but you tried even though you preferred the real world.

I know you wanted me to be more girly, more outgoing, more talkative, wear more lipstick, and stop saying fuck so much. Our relationship was complicated, but I know you were proud from a distance. Not because you wanted to be far away but because I was so hard to reach. You tried like hell to pull me in, get my attention, and find things we had in common. You never stopped trying. I am so grateful for that.

I'm hoping you don't stop now. This distance from you is something I have to do. You might not understand what I'm doing or why I'm doing it, but it makes sense to me. I know what I'm doing for Savannah and her future. I know the end goal. But I've veered off the traditional path to get there, so the road is rockier, overgrown, and much harder to walk. Sometimes I will have to stop, backtrack, fall into pits, climb back out, fly, fight, or run. No matter what, I must find—even create—my own pathway there and back. Please be there when I make it.

Wherever you are today, think of me and say a prayer. I'll be home soon.

S.

Chapter 1
Lighting the Match

The first time I saw my daughter's crystal blue eyes staring back at me from under her mass of wild, jet-black, monkey hair, it scared the hell out of me. The weight of her life was an eight-pound sack on my chest, and I could feel the pressure. She studied my face with intensity and must have wondered, "Who is this woman?" My inability to answer that question set off a fire alarm inside my head. Those eight pounds suddenly felt like a thousand.

The nurses swiftly carried her away for a bath as I limped to the restroom and said, "I'll be fine," to Mr. Husband. The room was empty now save the two of us, and we each played our roles effortlessly. He sat down and rested his head against the uncomfortable, green chair with a sigh as the door clicked shut.

Echoing his sigh, I squeezed the cold porcelain sink as I breathed in the bleach. I stared at myself in the mirror. The itchy hospital gown had been replaced by my stained, 4X, yellow sweats. They were the only thing that fit me. My eyes looked hollow and tired until I thought of my daughter, then they sparked to life. But if she was an extension of me and I was this 318-pound miserable woman in the mirror, then . . . I shut my eyes.

I could barely breathe.

For twenty-eight years, I had no identity other than the one assigned to me by friends, family, and society. Although it draped over me like a scratchy robe, I knew my loved ones cared about me and wanted to put me on the path that had been successful for them: marriage and children and happily-ever-after. So, I did what was expected.

But now it was evident to me that apart from motherhood, I was a very round, rebellious peg who had allowed myself to be shoved into a very square, docile hole. Whatever desires I had for my life had been locked away in my mind in favor of walking the prescribed straight and narrow. I was living someone else's idea of my life.

Looking in the mirror, I wanted for my daughter what I was desperately seeking for myself: choices. In the small town we lived in—as beautiful as it was—the choices for women were limited even beyond society's already narrowed view of what women could, or should, do.

If my daughter wanted to be a teacher, a stay-at-home mom, a nurse, or a secretary, that was fine by me as long as she chose her career path from a pile of one thousand options. But I didn't want her to pick from a pile of ten or a pile that I'd stacked for her or a pile that society said was okay. I wanted her to create her own pile of options from a life that gave her examples of what women could be outside of the standard fare typically prescribed for her gender.

"Whoa." I sat down on the toilet as the pain and blood loss of childbirth made me woozy.

"You okay?" asked Mr. Husband from outside the door.

"Can you help me to the bed?"

He helped me lie down between the cold, white sheets before lying down himself on the uncomfortable cot next to me and drifting off to sleep. I got no such peace. In the darkness, I swore that I would not leave anything about raising Savannah up to chance. I would be purposeful in my choices about every aspect of her life.

I clicked the call button and waited for the nurse to arrive.

"Yes, Stephanie?"

"I changed my mind. Please bring Savannah to my room. I'll just keep her in here."

"You sure? You need to rest, too."

Am I sure?

Thinking about her question for a second, I knew in my gut what I was going to do next and understood its implications. I accepted the fallout to come. If it meant Savannah would end up further along than I was, then it was worth it.

"I'm sure."

They brought her back to me as Mr. Husband stirred awake.

"Crazy hair." He laughed as he stretched.

I smiled. There was a gap between where I was in my life and where I wanted to be. If I didn't close that gap now when Savannah's life was just beginning, I would never close that gap. My daughter and I would be sucked into the quicksand of someone else's vision of our lives. And I couldn't let that happen. To her, to him, or to me.

* * *

A year later, I stared at the house Mr. Husband and I had shared. How could I walk away from the stability of a marriage, a home, and a preordained life for an uncertain future with no clear pathway?

I remember watching a documentary on Cindy Crawford shortly after my marriage began. When she was talking about divorcing Richard Gere, she said something like, "It was the first time in my life I realized you could love someone and not be married to them."

I asked for a divorce and knew what she meant.

Love does not disappear simply because the relationship does. And I did love him. But I was in my twenties and changing. He was in his twenties and changing. While he was becoming exactly the person he always wanted to be, I was just beginning to understand what I wanted out of life. My quarter-life crisis, ushered in by the most perfect human being I'd ever laid eyes on, forced a recognition of

10

the truth that Mr. Husband and I were growing apart and had been for quite a while. We were becoming the people we were meant to be, but those new people no longer fit, and I'm not sure they ever did. It wasn't that I didn't love him. I just loved Savannah more.

I wanted to be ready for the day when my daughter would ask me questions like, "What should I do with my life?" or "How do I know when it's the right person?" or "How do I make my dreams come true?" She'd want to know why I left her dad, why I support things like feminism and equality and environmentalism, why I vote the way I do, why sometimes things work and sometimes they don't, and why love hurts and why it feels good.

How was I going to answer her questions if I couldn't answer them for myself?

Who could Savannah be if I made all the right choices? Who could she be if I made the wrong ones? What could she lose if I made devastating ones? Her birth started a countdown in my head. There was only so much time, and what would I choose to do with it?

So, I left the house my husband and I had shared. After he had taken the few items he wanted, I packed every box, cleaned every corner, and threw out or donated the rest of my things. Five years disappeared in a matter of weeks. I took nothing with me except my daughter, my car, what was mine before we met, and a shared custody and support

11

agreement. If I was going to be bold enough to walk away and begin again, then it was imperative I do it on my own, make my own money, and earn my own way. There would be no alimony or keeping the house or making him pay for my life. This was my choice, and I had to own it. I would start from scratch, and we would both move on as free individuals, save the relationship he would have with his daughter.

When Savannah and I got to my mom's house that day, where we would stay for the short-term, my mother's face softened into a knowing expression. For the first time since I'd asked for the divorce, I broke down in tears, and she did not blame me for it.

I knew I was doing what was needed for me and Savannah, but knowing doesn't make it hurt less. I had committed to sharing a life with Mr. Husband. We shared a bedroom, laughs, tears, big blowup fights, and small meaningful moments. We swore to God and everyone that we would last. Saying goodbye to that wasn't easy, no matter how right the decision was. So, my mother held me tight, no matter how worried she was.

The next day, I got up and cashed in my mulligan. I was determined to make good decisions and bad decisions, as long as they were my decisions and mine alone. They would be unprescribed, wild, and only for me and my daughter. So that someday, when I stared in the mirror, I could look myself in the eye. So that when Savannah's stare pierced me as she asked the tough questions, I could answer them. And it wouldn't scare the hell out of me.

Chapter 2
Words as Swords and Shields

Journalism was the way out for me. It was the only place in my life where I felt powerful. The all-access press pass was alluring, but it was so much more than that. I was told I should have a voice in this world, and that it mattered. Not only was I paid to speak up but I was paid to ask hard questions, to use my words to fight for victims, and to give voice to those who had none.

It was an easy decision to support the two of us by picking up my pen and inking new beginnings for others as well as myself. It gave me the ability to hold others' monsters accountable even if mine ran free. It was an emotional release every time my words appeared in print.

Writing, in fact, had always been my go-to for finding peace in a world that was hell bent on telling me I was worthless. The careful crafting of words would ease the pain of my father calling me fat, ugly, and like my mother. Later, it was the way out of being bullied and teased by classmates. Inking the sentences helped me bleed out the memory of being molested by a family member. The paper in front of me was the shoulder to cry on.

It helped me move between fantasy and reality, escaping when I needed to and being present when I had to. My imagined world was the re-enactment of the real lives of other girls. They got to experience it. I had to conjure it. I was shut out of life and my own childhood, but I didn't understand why.

As a journalist, I could find those lost girls, and give them hope. I could find victims of racism and poverty and violence, and tell their stories. I could help serve justice by giving victims a chance to be heard. After a childhood cloaked in silence, this was my opportunity to remove the tape from my mouth and give voice to those marginalized in our society, myself included.

Through the process, I found I could not pick and choose which stories tugged at my heartstrings and which ones tore them to shreds. I only knew that after every story, my vision changed. Seeing the words in print made me realize the person had deposited a piece of themself into the lining of my soul. I was a chameleon, taking on the pigments of every story, good or bad, and making them part of my physiology, for better or worse. Their joy became my joy. Their love, my love. Their pain, mine.

Being a chameleon was a handy tool that allowed me to move in and out of people's lives easily. I didn't understand the duplicity it created inside me and its effect on others until I was well into my writing career. I started to realize people connected to me, but I could not return the favor. It wasn't just that my job required an objectivity that forced me to put a wall between myself and others, it was that I wanted it there. After years of neglect, ridicule, and mental and emotional abuse, the wall

15

was my friend, keeping the pain of human relationships at bay.

I could feel their disappointment when they tried to connect with me but I didn't reciprocate to the same level. I got close to them until the article was written and then I was gone. That's when they realized they had, perhaps, been slightly swindled by me. They had given me more than I had given them. I took their story, put it into the world, gave them a voice and platform, then I slipped away into the night like a thief, stealing from them the comfort of a new friend.

I was no friend; I was a writer. My brokenness was my gift. It allowed me to empathize with my subject. I was entrusted with the details of other people's most intimate tales of love, tragedy, heartbreak, and laughter. It was an honor to be invited into their script, to partake in writing a piece of it, and to occasionally act as a catalyst in changing the ending. But then, as quickly as I had come into their life to change it, I was gone without a word and on to the next.

It was overwhelming at times.

As a writer, the need for constant space and distance to look at a story, deconstruct it, make sense of it, and spew it out on paper was unrelenting. It meant sitting inside emotions that weren't always pretty in order to get the story right. It meant reliving the murders, the violence, the bad things, until the story was exactly as it should be. Then I would clean it up and write it again until it made sense to the world. And sometimes, it didn't make sense to the world. They'd be angry at me, tell me I was a horrible person, threaten me and my life. And then sometimes, they'd give me a shiny award.

This state of duality was par for the course as a working journalist. But it was also specific to me, an introverted writer with an extroverted personality. Right and left brained. Creative and analytical. Smart and dumb. Loved and hated. Angel and devil. Obedient and rebellious. Mother and daughter. Sinner and saint. There was always, on any given day, a war waging inside of me. Sometimes it was hard to hear the voice of reason above the dueling opposites in my head.

When they were too much, I would hole up for days on end, speak to no one, and feel relieved. It's contrary to what most people are like, generally. Most humans with souls tend to like being around and experiencing other humans. Writers, on the other hand, want to crawl inside your head, analyze you, observe you, assign you a role in the world, and then write about it in a way that may or may not piss you off.

Writers connect with you insofar as they can write about that connection. Writers don't have souls. They're not meant to. Writers have words. And the really great ones string them together in a way that gives soul to story. The writer's soul lives in the words they write, not the bodies they inhabit. The

17

writer constructs and deconstructs souls. Promises to bear yours. Promises to give you one. Promises to make sense of life when it falls apart around you. Writers exist to answer the call of the soul. A writer's first love is story. Everything else pales in comparison.

Except when Savannah was born.

She was the only exception. Hers was the only voice that could cut through the bullshit and give me clarity. If I put her at the forefront of my decisions, the world became crystal clear. Because of that, the work I was doing as a journalist became a muddy question mark in my head.

I began to sense that being a single mother and earning a living as a journalist would be much harder than I anticipated. In fact, I slowly realized it would be a downright fight—regardless of career—to live in a world that valued married more than single, men more than women, and money more than gumption. The more stories I wrote, the more victims I championed, the more my theory gained weight.

I left everything behind to give Savannah more. In the process, I inadvertently created for myself a demographic the world didn't value: the single, working mother. So, how the hell was I going to contend with that when the whole reason I left was to gain the thing I now didn't seem to have access to: choices?

Chapter 3
The Hunted

I looked at my daughter, with her piercing blue eyes and rolling curls, and knew she was a target. As a single, working mother, so was I. We both had bullseyes on our backs.

I had read and written the stories about pedophiles targeting the notoriously overworked and emotionally spent demographic known as the single mother. Pedophiles preyed on those weaknesses to gain access to the mother, become a father figure to the children, and then molest the children they had groomed. Online dating made the situation worse by providing greater and more frequent access to a wider swath of vulnerable people.

While I was deeply concerned about dating under these circumstances, I was even more fearful of the family members and friends who cozied up to my daughter. Statistically, more than 93 percent of victims under the age of eighteen know their abuser, according to rainn.org. RAINN (Rape, Abuse & Incest National Network) is the largest organization, at the time of this writing, in the United States working against sexual abuse and sexual violence across age and gender.

I know the dangers because I was one of their statistics. I was about eight years old when it happened to me. It was not a stranger who accosted me but a relative. He was old enough to know better.

The effect was the same as if it had been a stranger. My body was used without my permission. Not that I knew at that age what it meant to give permission. I knew only that it felt wrong.

It happened on a pleasant summer day when all the adults were swarming upstairs, along with my parents. It smelled like sunscreen, chlorine, and watermelon as the cool air conditioning brought down the heat. I was practicing my handstands against a wall in the basement. I wanted to be more like my cousin, who was good at dancing and gymnastics. I put my hands down on the floor and lifted my feet up and my shirt would tumble down. Hands down, feet up, shirt tumbles. Hands down, feet up, shirt tumbles. When my relative joined me, he watched intently. I ignored him because I was interested in only one thing: doing a better handstand. Hands down, feet up, shirt tumbles, and then it happened.

I felt his cold, dry hands pressed against my stomach before moving to my bare chest with a light, purposeful pressure. I could only see his dirty toes past the hem of my shirt near my head, but I could feel his presence and his hands on my body. After that, my mind goes dark. The next thing I remember was running up the stairs, scared, looking for my mother. Everything in between was a blur, open to interpretation, unknown in its exactness. There was only innocence followed by fear.

When I found my mother, I crawled on her lap and said nothing. I had no understanding of what happened to me, only that it scared me. He scared me, but most importantly, he was family. And if I had been taught anything in my eight years of life, it was family above all else, no matter what. Lie if I had to, bury it if I need to, but in no way should it ever slip out of my mouth what happened to me in the basement. The feeling that I had to hide the abuse behind a veil of secrecy was almost more destructive than the abuse itself.

It wasn't long after that incident when I found my father's stash of dirty magazines. I eyed the perfection of the women inside and marveled at how different they looked from me. They wore bright, red lipstick and their nipples stood at attention for no one in particular. They seemed to be waiting for something, eyeing the viewer with a vacant expression meant for anyone and no one. It seemed grotesque, and I was obsessed with their plasticity. Was this what I was supposed to do? Should I have been vacant and expressionless with my relative?

I crawled into my dark closet, took my clothes off, and recreated the poses in the magazine even though I didn't know what they meant. If I could be them, maybe that would change my life somehow. Change me somehow. Maybe it would make my father be nicer to me and stop calling me fat. I did feel powerful in those positions in the back of my closet. But, in the presence of all men, I felt weak. My relative made me feel weak. I put my clothes back on and climbed out of the darkness into the bright sunlight, eyes blinking.

There were two of me now. The girl in the closet and the girl in the light. I felt separated, somehow, from my body. One little girl loved books and creeks and animals. She was filled with joy, riding the fence like a trusty steed in the front yard, laughing at my brother's jokes, and running through the woods with abandon. The cool, fresh scent of nature hung in my nostrils long after the grass stains faded from my shoes. My soul felt like summer, and I was at peace.

The other girl was suddenly focused on her body and the way it looked and felt. This girl paid close attention when her elementary crush told her he wouldn't be her boyfriend because she was fat. And she paid special attention to how sweaty and uncomfortable her body felt when her relative walked in a room. But mostly, she worried that someone would find her posing in the closet and ask her why she was doing it and she wouldn't know how to answer.

Now, at thirty years old, it was all coming back to me as I looked at my daughter. I was terrified that she'd learn intimate knowledge of her body the way I did, against her will, and at far too early an age. No. She would understand that family is not to be valued above all else. And it is not always safe. In fact, the logic of family loyalty demands that we lose

22

our heads in favor of protecting the very people who hurt us the most. I would not allow it.

"Savannah, did anyone touch you inappropriately at daycare?" I'd ask as I scanned her arms and legs for bruising.

"What does that mean? In-propriate?" she asked with her eyes wide.

"It means these places," I said. And I pointed to my own private areas, explaining these places should not be touched by anyone. Not strangers, not teachers, not friends, not family. Especially not family.

"Okay, Mommy."

"If someone tells you I said it's okay, it's not okay. Okay?"

"Okay."

"Okay?"

"Okay."

I gave her safe people to call or talk to.

"Pick someone."

"Who, Mommy?"

"People who make you feel safe. People you can talk to. Not just me, either. You need safe people who aren't just me and your dad."

"Okay."

She thought about it for a long time but within an hour we had a short list of safe people that she could report bad things to, or even just talk to if she needed an ear. I recognized from my own experience that reporting something so personal could be hard to tell your mom. I couldn't tell mine—maybe Savannah couldn't tell me. At least now, there was someone, many someone's, who could hear her worst nightmares if needed.

Amid all this, I was cautiously dating again. I had always been overweight, and the dates were few and far between. But now I was divorced and ready to see what was out there. I was slowly but surely losing weight, and there were more opportunities.

This guy was new to me. We had just started seeing each other. He was six foot two, handsome, interesting, and physically strong. He came over for our third or fourth date. After Savannah was asleep, I let him in for what was, by any account, an innocuous date. He brought over *Star Wars: Return of the Jedi* on DVD, which he knew was one of my favorite movies. As the familiar scroll began, he kissed me. We'd kissed before and I'd liked it, so I welcomed it this time. But then something seemed to shift inside of him. The kiss went from easy and sweet to rough as his hand started to tighten first on my arm and then around my hair.

"Whoa," I said pulling away, as his grip loosened.

"Sorry," he smiled and kissed me again. This time, his hold got even tighter.

"Hey," I said, pulling away. "Maybe let's watch the movie."

"Fine," he said, letting his annoyance show through.

After a moment, I felt his other hand on my thigh and he leaned over with a gentle kiss, as if to apologize. I let him and he kissed me again, but this time, his grip on the back of my neck was so strong, I couldn't pull away.

"Come on," he said as his one hand squeezed my thigh and the other jerked my neck with brute force towards his crotch. "You know you want it, you tease."

"Stop!" I couldn't move my neck because of the force of his grip, but I could move my eyes to look toward Savannah's room. I wanted to make sure she hadn't heard. Couldn't see. I didn't want her to walk out. I was terrified that she would come to check on my scream and become a victim herself.

Jesus Christ, Savannah, don't walk out. Stay asleep, stay asleep, stay asleep.

"I said stop!" I tried to pull away again, using my hands against his thighs to push myself away from him, pounding his legs with my fists when I could, but every time I pulled away, he squeezed my neck harder and yanked me towards his crotch. His grip on my neck was so tight by this point that I thought he was going to break it.

"Do it!"

"No!" And this time, instead of pushing against him, I let my body go weak and leaned into him, which caused him to lose his hold on me. It was

25

counter-intuitive to lean into my attacker, but I had learned the trick from my ex-husband, and it saved me that night. I dropped my body down and away from his hand and jumped up. I grabbed my cell phone and dialed 911, but I didn't press the call button.

"Leave now or I'm calling the cops!" I held up my phone, using my body to block the hallway to my daughter's room.

"You're fucking crazy!" He started grabbing his stuff, huffing around like I'd done something wrong.

"Get out!"

"Crazy bitch!"

"Get out now!" I grabbed his shoes and phone and threw them out the front door.

"Fuck you!"

"Out!"

He finally left, and I slammed the door behind him. After locking everything possible, I went to the window and watched him screech away. I crossed my arms across my chest, barely able to breathe. Fear kept me frozen in place.

Later in my life, when the incident would worm its way into my consciousness with a need for release, I would tell only a few friends about it. I told them that I was tough, that I had fought, that I was scared, sure, but I stood up for myself. These were the things I was supposed to say to myself and others to know that I was okay. But to myself, alone in my mind, one single image would haunt me for the rest of my life: me, standing there, bleeding and bruised, unable to do anything except be afraid.

I ran to Savannah's room and cracked open the door—she was sound asleep. I closed her door, ran to the bathroom, and looked in the mirror. My face was flushed from fighting him, and my limbs started to feel sore as the adrenaline left my body. A little blood came out of my nose, but I wasn't sure how that happened. I grabbed some tissue and wiped it away.

I rolled my neck and shoulders to ease the strain while pulling up my hair to see the back of my neck. A deep, red handprint and fingernail grooves marked one side. My back felt sore, so I pulled up my shirt to see it. A bruise was already forming next to the red mark on my back. I couldn't tell what caused it.

I looked at my reflection again and saw the tears in my eyes as I covered my mouth with both hands and started to cry quietly so I wouldn't wake Savannah. The thin line between what happened and what could have happened was terrifying.

He could have broken my neck.

He could have raped me.

He could have killed me and went for Savannah.

So many women before me (and so many after), at different times, and at the hands of different men, had been and would be brutally injured, raped,

27

and murdered for not complying. I was lucky. And that knowledge was devastating.

Working as a crime and courts reporter, I knew the danger. Women hear these cautionary tales, and I'd even written some of them. All of them start the exact same way: the innocent connection, the building of trust, the nice guy façade to get in your home and then the worst possible nightmare. Women just like me dating men just like him and our children in the middle of it all.

What the fuck just happened?

Before I was assaulted, I thought a situation like this would be black and white. I would know it was coming, but even if I didn't, I would know exactly what to do when it was over. It would be easy to call the police and report a guy like him. But after my assault, I was more confused than anything else. When I looked back on it, it felt like time stopped. It felt like an hour of total confusion and chaos. In real time, it probably lasted less than five minutes, but I had absolutely no concept of time or its passing.

Seriously, what the fuck just happened?

The solution was simple: I would not bring anyone to my home again while Savannah was there. I would not introduce anyone to Savannah. I would limit my dating pool to only those men I worked with or knew in a capacity that I was comfortable with. I would have sex on my own time, while Savannah was at her dad's house. I would keep men at a distance. Sifting through the bad ones to find the

28

good one was not worth mine or my child's life. I didn't need to find The One; I would be my own one and find my own way. And I would protect my daughter in the process.

Still, it didn't seem fair that I had to rearrange my life because a man felt entitled to my body even though I owed him nothing. Now, in addition to all the other things I had to contend with as a single mother, a man's violence was somehow also my problem. It felt like I was bearing the brunt of something I shouldn't have to.

I was a single woman who wanted to date. But while men could just go about their lives, date, get remarried, and be secure, I had to shut down my desire for an intimate relationship to protect my child. I felt I couldn't date as a normal single woman because I was not a normal single woman. I had a daughter. A female child. And she was even more vulnerable than I was. I felt like I had to defend us both from a world that placed all the burden of safety on victims instead of predators.

Weighing on my mind long after the incident was also the fact that I never reported it. Just like after I'd been molested, I couldn't speak. In the moment, in both cases, there was fear. As an adult, I was scared what Mr. Date Rape might do to me outside the confines of a police station or a courtroom. The police couldn't stand guard 24-7, restraining orders were virtually unenforceable (and a joke), and I had Savannah to think about. There was also the issue of what to report. What had happened to me, really? I defended myself against a bad guy.

What am I reporting? My inability to discern a rapist from a normal guy?

That led to the feeling of stupidity. What warning signs I had missed? Surely, there had been something. He must have given off something that should have sent up a red flag, right? But there had been nothing right up until the moment when there was something. It was zero to sixty in a matter of seconds. His normal guy deception was perfectly practiced and brilliantly executed.

If I couldn't keep such beasts out of my home, with all the journalist knowledge I had, how in the hell would Savannah? I was doing all this work to help her protect herself, but now I was recognizing that in the end, if a man wants to dupe a woman, he can and will. In that very painful moment when she realizes she's been had, it will be too late. She'll either be dead or she'll be alive and criticized for not knowing better. In the worst case, she'll be both dead and criticized.

I was exhausted, and I wanted it to just be over. I didn't want to talk or share about it ever again. I didn't even want to think about it. I felt lucky to be alive. Lucky to not have been raped six feet from where my child was sleeping. The feminist in me— the reporter in me—wanted to call the police. But the little girl in me was still wearing tape over her mouth.

The only way to even attempt to save our lives was to recognize one very small fact specific to women: Savannah and I were prey. We were the hunted. And to survive, we would have to learn how to play defense because no one was preventing men from playing their dangerous offense.

So, the next round of teachings had a bit more physicality. I taught her how to kick out a taillight if she got thrown in a trunk, I taught her how to kick a guy in the balls and gouge his eyes with her thumbs. I taught her how to look under her car and in the backseat before she gets in to drive and how to lock the doors after. I taught her to scream. And in the meantime, I kept looking for the classes that were teaching boys not to molest, beat, rape, and murder women in the first place.

Of course, I never saw any of those.

And when the day was done, and the training complete, I read her a bedtime story and waited until her eyes got heavy as she fell fast asleep with her shiny curls covering her pillow. That's when I started my nighttime routine. I locked all my doors and windows, shut all the shades, slid a butcher knife under my pillow and left my phone on 911 as I drifted off to sleep with the hope that someday the constant fear of being an animal of prey would leave me.

Chapter 4
Murder in a Small Town

Sitting in my car outside of Savannah's daycare center, I pulled out a picture of Harper from my work bag. What a lovely five-year-old girl she had been. Her bright eyes sparkled under the magic of fancy lighting and glamour makeup. It must have been a fun day for her and her family. She loved to play dress-up and pretend to be her mother or a rock star or a pageant queen. I smiled thinking how happy she must have been the day that photo was taken.

I was writing the story of her death to keep her murderer behind bars, and I couldn't look at my daughter the same after reading Harper's police files. I poured over everything from the investigation. All the documents characterized Harper's murder as "satanic." She had been raped. Shot. Disemboweled.

I stared at the crisp edges of her photo as tears stung my eyes and sickness set in. It was a sealed moment in time, never to have any photo follow it. The depths of this little girl's tragic death were unimaginable for any parent. The horrific details were too graphic to grasp. Her young life cut short by a predator.

Staring at the day care center, I knew I had to leave. I had to go do my job but wondered at what cost? My decisions bore a chain reaction that had a direct impact on my daughter. I couldn't help but think of Harper's parents making these same decisions. They were going to work, making a living, socializing, and trusting the world around them. If they didn't the fear would eat them alive. The same thing all parents do. Then, a monster shook the foundation of their very lives, stealing this little girl with bright eyes and leaving them with a string of "what ifs" and "could have beens."

I gripped the steering wheel as I slowly inhaled and exhaled, trying to ground myself. I had to will myself out of the parking lot and back to work. But all I could think of was, "Will she be okay if I go?"

In Savannah's first three months of life, I practically glued the baby monitor to my ear, listening for her breath and making sure she hadn't succumbed to SIDS. I would double-check the mattress and make sure her stuffed animals hadn't accidentally made their way into her crib. I was vigilant. When the time came for her to sleep alone through the night, I let her cry her way through it, but not without my trusty monitor. It was her first taste of independence.

Now, she was growing and becoming more independent, and I was sending her out into the world and believing she would be okay.

I stared at Harper's picture.

Could the same world that brutally brought this child's life to an end be trusted with my daughter?

33

While I was writing their story, Harper's grandma had invited me into her home, which was a warm space with lovely furniture and lots and lots of family pictures on the walls. She and her husband talked about their granddaughter and what they imagined she could've been. Their memory of her as a child let them imagine the possibility of a life that would never be realized by her, by them, by anyone.

It felt like a hollow victory to keep the murderer in prison after the fact rather than preventing the murder itself. Of all the powerful things my pen could do, rewriting their past wasn't one of them. And more than anything, I wanted to rewrite that brutal night for them. But that wasn't real life. And I knew all too well how easy it was to open a door for a monster and welcome them in. And now, the rest of their lives would be defined by only two chapters—the chapter before Harper was murdered and the chapter after.

I was humbled by how brave they were to talk about their pain, to rehash such horrific memories of a time they'd rather forget to pay tribute to Harper's memory. This was their way of rewriting that night and saving others from a similar fate.

Others like my daughter.

An uneasiness crept along the hairs of my neck as I sat in their living room.

Who had I hurt by not being brave enough to report the monsters in my life?

34

I smiled politely at them and began shifting my weight from hip to hip as I moved from sitting on their couch to standing. My breath felt trapped as though it couldn't escape the confines of my throat.

"Th-thank you for having me."

I leaped for the door, the walls closing in on me too fast to manage. I got in my car and sucked on the air, trying to extract as much oxygen from it as I could to keep me steady. Instead, I just got a little woozy until I finally caught my breath.

I would never forget Harper's sweet face.

The county sheriff who helped me with Harper's story told me that no one who worked the case that night was ever the same again. They were all haunted by the memory of what they had seen and heard. I would never be the same again, either. The nightmares persisted long after the ink of Harper's story had dried.

I had always told my daughter I loved her. Now, I told her every day, hugged her for no reason, took more photos than necessary. A dirty glass from Savannah's lunch and one over-used game piece sat in my drawer next to a lock of her hair just in case her fingerprints or DNA samples were needed. A bag in my closet held those little DNA kits from every daycare and elementary school she'd ever attended. And sometimes I'd hold her for just a little too long to remember her smell, in case remembering was all I had.

The decisions in my life were now divided into two chapters—the decisions I made before Harper and the ones I made after. I had to revisit the question of my career: Who and what was I inviting into my and Savannah's lives by being an investigative journalist?

I began to shy away from certain stories that were assigned to me. I started to take less risks, so much so, that my editor at the time had to go on a stakeout with me because I made excuses not to go. I didn't want to put myself in the line of fire and risk losing my life or my daughter's life. Once the fear found me, I could no longer do investigative reporting in the manner it deserved.

I didn't know how to tell the people who saw this dramatic shift in me that Harper's death had rewritten something inside me. Harper died when she just five years old. She didn't get to be a dancer or a singer or even a child. She didn't get to fulfill any of her dreams. Her death forced me to face my own mortality. It forced me to face my daughter's mortality too.

I began applying for jobs in Columbus that were with lifestyle magazines or part of a communications team at a larger company. I knew I wanted to write, but I no longer knew in what capacity.

A few months later, I got a job offer in Columbus, Ohio, for an editing position at a lifestyle magazine. It was more money than I had made to date; it was a much easier role, topic-wise; and it allowed me to make a jump to a bigger city with more choices and opportunities for both Savannah and me.

This was the next chapter I needed. I packed my bags, and we set off to Ohio's central city. I owed it to Savannah and myself to keep moving forward on our journey. I owed it to Harper.

Chapter 5
Suicide Watch

I didn't know how deeply dark and disturbing my thoughts had become until the knife nearly pierced my thirty-three-year-old skin. After two years in Columbus, I was curled in a ball on my bathroom floor believing that death would be better than the life I was living. It seemed there was nothing more for me to offer the world and that my daughter, the one person I had changed my life for, would be better off without me.

The anguish inhabiting my body continued to work its way through my system the next evening as I sat on a bench outside my apartment complex. The twilight hour cast its blue on me as Savannah threw breadcrumbs at the ducks. She was innocently unaware of the profoundly turbulent emotions inside of me as she laughed at the bullfrogs croaking to their mates across the pond. Rubbing my wrists raw, I remembered the last few months of my life. The memories elicited a dry laugh from my throat as I thought of how inadequate I was even at suicide.

This was not the first time I had put a knife to my wrist. After thoughtful consideration over many years, the knife became my preferred tool of self-destruction. Since my stepfather was an avid hunter, there were plenty of guns in the house to choose from. But I remembered a story about a man who tried to kill himself with a shotgun, blew off the

38

side of his head, and lived, which felt like something I would do, so that was out of the question.

Pills were also a consideration, given the pharmacy living in our kitchen cabinets. My family (comprised mostly of medical professionals) believed strongly that there wasn't a condition that a pill couldn't fix. I believed in natural approaches to healing. My approach to death wasn't going to include pills, either. So, that was out.

No, a knife would feel like a paper cut, and once I bled out to a certain point, I'd pass out. That would happen quickly, and I wouldn't remember anything else. Even if I managed to survive, I'd have only the scar and little memory of the trauma. And maybe, just maybe, I'd even get the help I clearly needed.

Not that anyone thought I needed help. Society expected me to just get over it and buck up. Family members would say, "You don't mean it when you say you're depressed." Friends would say, "You'll be fine. Stop whining." I didn't argue with them. The first time depression hit me, I was only a teenager with no experience about why I felt this way. So, they knew more than me, right?

The second time, I was a freshman at the University of Akron and a pre-med major. Those courses appealed to me because I liked taking care of people, and I enjoyed science and physics as they related to the body and movement. And because of my family's medical background, this major—unlike

39

writing or anything creative—was given more encouragement and support. In their mind, medicine was familiar, it was guaranteed income after college (people will always be sick), and they had plenty of contacts to offer me in the field. Creative fields, of course, offered none of these things.

Campus life was exciting and terrifying. My newfound freedom was liberating, but the unexplored territory of a college campus was stressful. I'd eat lunch by myself in the dorm room instead of conquering the fear of no one sitting with me in the cafeteria. Making new friends felt excruciating and looking for a boyfriend was so far out of my reach it seemed impossible.

Drugs and alcohol were the first things offered to me for coping with the difficulty of transitioning from home to college life. Waking up on a fraternity porch with no idea how I got there happened a couple times. Then one night, a frat boy had to stop his brother from trying to rape me while I was semi-unconscious. He walked me home, and I never went back. But I did not stop drinking or smoking pot. I found that cigarettes and oral sex were most helpful for calming my racing mind.

All of these things were how I dealt with having strange attacks where my heart would tick up a notch, my palms would sweat, my mind would race, and I couldn't concentrate. These same attacks had started around age fifteen and were most pronounced during times of significant change in my life. I didn't know what they were, but I knew that after they were done, I'd feel tired and depressed.

I remember having them when I was talking to my parents about UCLA and moving to California after high school to be an actress. Every time I talked about pursuing my dreams on the West Coast, I'd have these episodes. They got so intense I had to forego the California talk and stay closer to home. I'd initially thought that moving to Akron had solved that problem, but now it seemed like nothing had resolved the feelings behind the attacks. But smoking a cigarette after oral sex in a Wendy's parking lot took the edge off for a few blissful seconds before the attack would come back ten times stronger.

By Homecoming I was failing my pre-med classes and hiding it well from my parents. As it turns out, when you're trying to numb your emotions, you're also numbing your brain cells and any inclination to do well at anything. The letter from the registrar that I was going to be placed on academic probation was anti-climactic. I would have been disappointed in the University if they hadn't threatened to kick me out. One more semester to clean up my act, they said, and then I was gone.

The serrated edges of a sharp knife I stole from the cafeteria rehearsed practice run after practice run on my ivory wrists across bright blue veins.

Is the cut vertical or horizontal to really make it bleed? When will my roommate be back?

41

She needed to be gone long enough for me to bleed out or else it would be one more thing I failed at. There was also the issue of the note.

Should I leave one? What would it say?

My heart pounded and my breathing became erratic. One of those attacks I hadn't yet given a name to grabbed at my throat as my mind raced. My hands shook as I stared at them in utter confusion.

What's happening to me?

I dropped the knife into the trash and jumped up to look in the mirror at my pale reflection and trembling lips. My fingers touched my face just to make sure I was real and not a ghost. I called my mom, who put my stepdad on speaker phone with her. The conversation was robust with a note of, "You'll be fine" and a hint of, "You just want attention."

They were concerned, of course, but given my gregarious personality, it was hard for them to understand I could be anything less than cheerful and put together.

So, that was that.

A few months later, I transferred to Muskingum University, back to my hometown, and the attacks abated for a bit. But when I got married a few years after graduating, they came back with a vengeance. Within the first year of blissful nuptials, I found myself sitting on a cold, steel table in the doctor's office. I was exhausted and numb.

"I'll prescribe you Xanax," he said as though this was the end all be all solution to what was ailing me.

I was hoping for a physical ailment. An explanation from my doctor that I could touch, feel, and manipulate.

But the doc said matter-of-factly, "It's your mind."

Fuck.

Seeing how my father's anxious behavior devastated our family, I hated that I was trapped by the same struggle. Never knowing when a panic attack would snipe me in the middle of just living my life was an overwhelming and disruptive ordeal every single day.

So, the doctor gave me pills and sent me home with the news that I would battle anxiety for the rest of my life. He said medication would help ease the anxious reaction to whatever was the trigger of my many bad days and nights.

The phrase, "Whatever was the trigger," stuck with me. My college degree was in English and psychology. The classes I took informed my opinion that most adverse behaviors stem from a triggering event or a series of triggering events. While I knew that many brain conditions were improved by medication, some can be solved by changing your life and changing how you react. Not knowing what else to do, I took the Xanax. An hour later, I felt buzzed. And I hated that.

One late night, I stumbled upon an infomercial for a program that promised cognitive and behavioral methods for managing anxiety as opposed to medication.

I watched that program with my mother's skepticism. Healing anxiety and depression with a workbook and some tapes? *Yeah right.* And doing it without medication? *Pfft.*

"My mom would think that's stupid," I said to myself.

I stared at the phone number and the pills for at least five minutes. I got out of bed, took them both to the bathroom, and held them over the wastebasket, weighing the option in each hand.

"Sorry, Mom." I tossed the pills into the wastebasket and leaned into my own opinion of what would fix me.

Two weeks later, my twenty-four-year-old eyes stared at the workbook in front of me. It was asking me to take all the pain in my brain and put it into ink. To take abstract thoughts and make them real. To take all the bad things I had buried and unearth them for the world to see. As I touched the clean, barren white space of the pages, the vastness of that request set my heart racing. An attack was coming again. It was a strong one. It caused blurry spots to appear on the thick, blank pages. I closed my eyes, trying to clear my vision as sweat seeped from my pores.

My heart ticked up another notch.

Breathe, Stephanie, breathe.

It felt like a line of ants was marching up my arms, first mounting an offense on my fingertips, then battling across my hands. Numbness followed their trail up my shoulder and into the side of my face, as though a stroke was taking over my body.

Come on, now, breathe.

My heart was banging against my rib cage. Sweat dripped down my face as I impulsively reached for the phone. My fingers traced the numbers 911, 911, 911.

One more time.

911.

I closed the workbook, held the phone to my chest, and curled into a ball as I waited for it to pass. Would it be ten minutes today or sixty?

"Deep breaths," I whispered to myself. "Breathe, Stephanie. Breathe."

The panic attack ripped through my body. My subconscious gnawed on me, strangling my brain with a barrage of fearful thoughts, flooding my body with adrenaline, and forcing the oxygen out. My mind was, quite literally, attacking my body.

Deep breaths, Stephanie.

My body was weeping with exhaustion. The attacks forced me to become a shut-in, trapped in my own home. But more specifically, I was trapped in my own body. And more painfully, trapped in my own mind. No one could get through. My family tried

45

but the ailment was hidden in the depths of my mind in a place no one could touch, help, or heal.

Now here I was, curled up in a ball in front of the closed workbook, having a panic attack with the pills at the bottom of the garbage can.

Just facing those blank pages turned out to be a task in and of itself. Whatever was buried in the dark corners of my head was festering and causing me to turn into this shell of a person. If I let it out, what additional harm was it going to do? How else was it going to destroy my life? Or worse, someone else's? But maybe if I dug it out by its roots, it would change me for the better.

I crawled out of my ball, steeled myself against the waves of panic, and started to write down answers to the stinging questions it asked about my childhood, my memories, my pain, my happiness, and all the characters who played a role in each of those things. I started to dig deep into the spaces of my mind where the darkness was hiding and shine a light onto what had been slowly killing me.

Somehow, someway, my answers always led to the same place: I had been silent my whole life about the bad things that happened to me in favor of being the good girl who would just take it.

I remember loving when my mother would say, "You're such a good girl, Stephanie."

A good girl.

Hearing that was the only time I felt more special than my Golden Child brother, who could do no wrong. He was athletic; he was funny; he was, most importantly, a he. He was loved by everyone, on both sides of the family, and I was the leftover. He was the first son and the first grandson on my mom's side. He did everything first, so by the time I was born, it had all been done before.

My entire life I had listened to my family members praise my brother and my cousins my entire life. I stood watching on the sidelines as everyone in my family got homecoming crowns and state titles and fancy military awards. Instead of being special, I was always the one cheering on the special people.

But what was special about me?

The only way for me to compete was to be a good girl. I always played by the rules. And I was richly rewarded for being pleasing, passive, proper, and perfect. By virtue of my own need for attention, I had become the very picture of an obedient child. So much so, that on the rare occasion when I would rebel, the punishment would be swift and fierce. Living like a rag doll made everything easier.

Weeks later, I stared at the workbook's no longer blank pages, which were filled with stories of the past featuring ghosts that hung around longer than they should have. Those scrawled pages were filled with realizations, understandings, anger, fear, and loathing. From those chicken-scratched notes, I learned what my anxiety triggers were. I learned how to break the panic cycle. I learned where the poison was stemming from. Most of it anyway.

I had been suffering from the effects of sexual, emotional, and mental abuse, in addition to bullying and mistreatment. The anxiety was stemming from a lack of knowledge about how to properly address the bad things that had happened to me. As a result, my insides had been rewritten in a way I was no longer willing to accept.

The scary stuff was finally out of my brain and on the pages. Once my thoughts became ink, I could somehow control them. Manipulate them into something tangible that I could mold into a better reality.

For the first time in three months since the panic attacks started, I stood with a straightened spine and walked out my front door. The anxiety wasn't gone and never would be. But for the first time since I'd said, "I do," I was able to manage it. After a couple more months, I was done with all the tapes, books, and workbooks. I started channeling my anger into strength.

Then Savannah was born, and that new strength allowed me to change my life in a way that would give my daughter opportunities I never had. My hope was that it would prevent her from having a workbook full of dangerous ideas about herself.

* * *

I wish I could say that was the end, but since anxiety never leaves you, the attacks didn't stay suppressed for long. Sadly, my desire to kill myself erupted again in Massillon, Ohio, after the divorce when the full weight of single motherhood came bearing down on me. It reared its ugly head again just a few years later, in Columbus. While the landscape had changed, the circumstances hadn't. As a single mother, I struggled financially every single day, going from bounced check to bounced check and from power shut off to power shut off. While I was thinner, I still hadn't reached my goal. And as Savannah got older, she needed me more not less.

It has to get better, right? I mean, it has to.

That's about when the twisted feelings of anxiety and depression lurched from my insides and landed me on the bathroom floor again with tears streaming down my face. The pattern had emerged. Every time I tried to make a major change in my life, the anxiety would flare up, I'd back off, and then I'd be depressed for missing an opportunity. The vicious cycle wore me down to my bones.

My doctor recommended anti-depression medication instead.

Always with the pills. Any time I mentioned my anxiety or depression, the first thing a doctor would do is put a prescription for this pill or that one in my hand. Do pills work? Sometimes. Are they necessary for some? Absolutely. But a pill will not fix the ups and downs of being a single parent.

49

"Mommy, I'm hungry, why don't we have cereal?" *I don't have money to buy it.*

"Stephanie, your electric bill is due. Pay it today or face disconnection." *I can overdraw my account and get groceries later.*

"Mommy, will you read to me?" *Yes, of course. But it has to be a short one because I'm falling asleep even though it's only seven o'clock at night.*

"Stephanie, you need to come to the family reunion. Everyone wants to see Savannah." *I don't have gas money to drive there.*

"Mommy, change my diaper." *I need to start potty-training.*

"Stephanie, this story sucks! Write it again." *I do suck. Where's the candy?*

"Hey, I'm getting remarried. And we want Savannah in the wedding." *Your new wife is not to be called Mom. That is my title, and mine alone.*

"Stephanie, your day care money was due last week. I need it by Friday or Savannah has to leave." *I can open a new checking account and use that money to pay for day care. I'll cover the other account later.*

"Steph, come out drinking with us!" *Uh, I can't, Savannah is sick. (They don't need to know I can't afford a babysitter or even a beer).*

"Mommy, why are you exercising when it's dark out." *Midnight is the first chance I had to do it, kiddo. Go back to bed. I love you.*

"Stephanie, call your mother back. I've called you six times!" *I'M BUSY.*

"Mommy, why are the lights off?" *Oh, um . . . they're working on a line, honey. Don't worry. Mommy will fix it.*

"Hey sexy, can I come over?" *Fuck. You.*

I was physically spent, emotionally depleted, mentally exhausted, and financially destitute. A pill wasn't going to fix that.

Every decision I made felt like I was only putting out the closest fire. But there were always others. How to get my work done while tending to a sick child, or should I buy groceries versus gas, or should I overdraw my checking account to buy medicine, or do I buy brakes for my car or gasoline, or do I skip getting my cavity filled so I can pay for daycare this month, etc. My decisions felt suffocating, like choking on smoke while the flames crisped my skin.

Our lives felt bleak, which wasn't what I expected. I was also isolated. No one could help me with the unexpected sick days or the unexpected school closings or the unexpected anything that comes with having a child. And that was unexpected.

I was alone, making life-altering decisions sometimes up to thirty times a day with little guidance. The advice I got from my well-meaning mother and other family members was always, "Move back home. We'll take care of you until you

51

get back on your feet." That was the exact opposite of what I needed or wanted to do.

To them, it was obvious that I needed help, and they would help me if . . . It was that "if" part that always got me. They would help me only if I moved back to a place that was convenient and if I made the decisions they wanted me to make. But that was the reality I had escaped, and I didn't want to go back. I didn't want to be pleasing to anyone anymore. I wanted my own life.

I just didn't realize that getting my own life would look like this.

Fuck.

I stared at my wrists some more and noticed the bright blue veins. I had good veins. Good, strong veins. Good, strong hands. My body was strong now, thanks to the weightlifting. They say that when the body is strong, the mind is strong. There's something to that.

But the number of times my body had been violated, mocked, and objectified, always made me feel disconnected from its beauty. There was nothing beautiful about molestation, sexual assault, and endless body shaming. My mind had always told me lies about how dirty I was, how unworthy I was, and that my body was to blame for that.

But through running and strength training, I had successfully reverse-engineered that connection and linked my body to my mind. I began hearing a different message than the one that had been on loop for almost thirty years.

In that moment on the floor, my body said to my mind, "You are strong and capable. Your body is yours and no one else's. The only thing dirty about you is how sweaty you are from kicking ass in the gym today. So, put the knife down. Because we're not done yet."

I picked myself up off the floor and stared at my reflection in the mirror.

I could kill myself, yes. But, while it would be a relief for me from a world that had routinely spit me out, it would have devastating consequences for the one person who had inspired me to become more—my daughter. Who would she become if I let her down like that? None of the forces against me seemed as bad as my child losing me to suicide.

My other option was to do what everyone else wanted me to do. I could move back home into the comfort zone I had escaped. There, everyone could say, "Good girl Stephanie. You made the right decision." They would pat me on the head for being so pleasing and accommodating. Like a good girl should be.

No.

I couldn't move back home. If I did, it would be my last move, and that felt like a death sentence too. I would still be killing myself, just in a different way.

I stared at my swollen eyes and dripping nose in the mirror.

Stay. Fight for your life.

My blue veins pumped with relief as the knife dropped from my fingers and clinked against the porcelain sink.

And now I was watching my daughter play by the pond. In the twilight, the bullfrogs were loud as I sat on the bench outside my apartment. I was tired and pale but knew deep down that I had come too far to turn back now. It didn't matter where I was going. It only mattered that I wouldn't go back.

Uncertainty echoed loud and clear in my mind. This was harder than I'd imagined it would be. Much harder. I didn't know how I was going to get through the next day or the next week. I didn't know how I was going to keep the lights on or food on the table. But I knew I was strong enough now to figure it out. In that moment, new steel was inserted in my spine.

It was the last time I ever held a knife to my wrist.

Chapter 6
The Prodigal Father

A major blizzard hit on my daughter's fifth birthday. She was two hours away at my parent's house where her father had dropped her off following his custody weekend. Fields of white powder that were more than a foot high in all directions. Every level of emergency had been issued by the county, and I had no idea how I was going to get to her. But I told her I'd come, and I was going to keep that promise.

The roads, as any reasonable person would expect, were closed because of the storm. While the road crews had been able to clear the bulk of the hefty snow off the interstate, according to the news, they hadn't yet gotten to the last few inches, so driving conditions didn't get any better the further east you got. East was where I needed to go.

It's her birthday.

I could feel my promise weighing as heavily on my heart as the snow on my Ford Explorer. Staying home would be easy. Acceptable. Demanded, even, from the Highway Patrol. No one would blame me for staying safe in my warm apartment.

But I made her cake.

I shut off the television and got the snow shovel out of the closet.

I'll just dig out the car and clean it off.

I put on my snow boots and opened the door. Thirty minutes later I hopped in my car.

I'll just warm up the car. You're supposed to do that in cold weather anyway.

The engine jumped to life.

Hmmm…maybe I'll just put her cake and presents in here, too. And keep the car running. For the engine to stay warm, of course.

I ran inside and grabbed the cake, presents, and a sparkly princess crown, then headed back out.

Maybe I'll just try to get to the Interstate.

Thirty-five minutes later, I was about five miles down Interstate 315 when I saw the sign for I-70 East. I took a deep breath.

I'm going.

For eighty miles I crept slowly but steadily along I-70. At times, I drove the only vehicle in sight for miles and miles of snow and nothing else. No lines were keeping me straight, no signs were visible, and no landmarks were discernible. I was driving blind, white knuckled, and stressed, relying on my instincts about where I was to make it to my parents' house. It was a stupid thing to do. But I had promised my daughter.

I pulled into their driveway four hours later. The arduous journey melted away the minute I saw Savannah's face. When she opened the door, all she knew in that moment was that mom had delivered. Whatever I had to go through to get there didn't matter to this small child who put her absolute faith in me. She just wanted me there. And I showed up.

The next morning, on our ride home after the Interstate became drivable, I felt something rotten bubble up from inside me. Just like Savannah, I had waited many times in my childhood for my father to arrive. Face pressed to the glass, hand on the phone, waiting. Always waiting. Seeing her face light up at my arrival gave me so much joy. It also elicited a crushing pain for the little girl I was. The one who was still waiting. Knowing how much I'd sacrifice to keep my promises to my daughter, suddenly underscored how little my father had given up for me.

I always knew that my life was, in some ways, an afterthought. My parents had my brother and then divorced. My mom went back to my dad and remarried him. I was born out of the second union between them. I always thought I was the thing that came as a result of grasping at straws for a second chance that never should have been. It seemed like I was a reminder to my father of where his life took a wrong turn. He never said it quite that way, but he said other cruel things that made me feel like it was true.

Whatever anger I held toward my father was the result of a little girl who loved her father more than her father loved her. Whatever grief I had to contend with grew directly from waiting for my dad to show up. It didn't have to be magical or memorable, he just had to come to the door.

But he never really did.

On a few occasions, he'd pick us up or we'd go to his mom's house, but for the most part, he just wasn't around. In contrast, my stepfather was a constant presence. He had the tough conversations and the fights but also showed the love and support. He went to all my basketball and volleyball games. We still love to laugh about the high school volleyball game where the referee pulled me and the coach aside between matches and said, "If your dad doesn't stop yelling at the referees for bad calls, he's going to have to leave."

I ran to the stands and laughed as I whispered to him and my mom, "Thank you. But, seriously, stop yelling at the refs!" I have no such memories with my real father. But what does "real father" mean anyway when it comes to who raises and loves you?

Now I looked at my daughter, and I saw in her eyes the need for my attention and approval. My heart broke a little knowing I had looked at my father the same way many times. I'd been wide-eyed and hopeful for love from someone who could never, would never, give it. It caused the chasm between us to grow over the years. I could never reconcile the notion that the man who was a stranger gave me the love and support that I needed when the man who was my blood did not.

What if Savannah couldn't forgive me for my mistakes?

I remembered how I'd yelled at her the day before. The week before. The month before. The year before. And the year before that. When she started to crawl and tried to put her finger in an electrical outlet in a house that wasn't baby-proofed, I had screamed so loud it terrified her. Her eyes were wide with tears and confusion about why her mother, who had just kissed and loved her up, now had a face distorted in anger and fear.

I winced in pain at the memory and wondered how many more mistakes I was going to make as a parent.

Would she see me the same way I saw my father?

I wanted to forgive him. Because when I looked in the mirror, I could see him in me. I was a writer, and he could write too. I was successful in athletics like he was. We both laughed at the little things. I was as much him as I was my mother. The traits I had come to value in myself, I couldn't help but value in him. To reject him was like rejecting a piece of myself, denying a piece of my existence because it didn't suit me. Rejecting it didn't make it go away.

On the other hand, I also bore his worst traits. My words were like knives in a heated argument, cutting out your heart in a second. I'd inherited his maddening way of sinking into himself

59

when he failed to understand how to deal with a frustrating situation. His anxious behaviors had become mine, and I knew how disruptive it could be.

He was broken.

And I, of all people, understood broken.

As I watched my daughter sleep, I tried to remember some of the better moments my brother and I had with my father before he wrote himself out of our lives. Not because I wanted to, but because I needed to. It was the only way the darkness of his absence could be kept at bay, the same way a sunrise pushes night to the other side of the world.

Pizza was the first thought that came to mind. My brother and I spent a few nights with our father over pepperoni pies after the divorce. My grandma's house was also a big part of my past with my father. They hosted Sunday dinners, which I loved, and a few times we went to my grandma's house for the Fourth of July. My dad and his brother would shoot fireworks off in the backyard. We'd all watch from the screened-in porch and laugh as the reds, greens, and whites would light up the sky.

As I brushed a hair away from my sleeping daughter's face, tears stung my eyes. I watched her quietly for a moment.

I am different from my father.

The man who made up half of my gene pool might have cared if I put my finger in a socket, or if my heart was broken at sixteen, or twenty-five, or thirty-one. He just hadn't cared enough to be present.

60

My mother was the one who read the books, made
the dinners, and mended the hearts. She was tough,
but she was there, even when it was hard. My mother
wore a badge of honor my father would never be able
to claim. My stepfather had a similar badge, showing
up for our everyday activities, paying for college,
giving us a home.

Because my father had so consistently
underachieved at being present in our lives, I became
an overachiever, putting an unreasonable amount of
pressure on myself. The pain of his absence was like
molten lava that would erupt in the strangest ways, at
unexpected times, and with a ferociousness even I
didn't understand.

Worse, no elixir could fix me. No cure could
rid my soul of what my father had sewn into me. He
had, from early on, woven into the very fabric of my
existence his disdain for me. To start with, I was a
girl. Then I was a girl who was too fat. Then too
ugly. Then worthless. And then nothing. He
apologized to me once for all the times he called me
fat. He said it was wrong of him. But hearing an
apology so many years after the fact did little to
remove the venom he'd injected into my blood. And
worse, I couldn't tell if what hurt me more were his
painful words about how fat I was and that no one
would love me or the fact that he was (mostly) right.

By the time Savannah was a pre-teen, we
made one final visit to try and connect with my
father. When we got there, I looked around the small

61

living room at all the photos in it. Photos of my brother and nephew were everywhere. There were none of me or Savannah. He had obliterated us from his life in all forms.

On the ride home, Savannah asked of the photos, "Did you notice?"

"I did."

"Does it bother you?"

I thought about her question for a moment.

"It used to," I said. I shrugged. "But it just doesn't anymore."

That was the last time I ever referred to him as Dad.

The girls I grew up with who had fathers who saw nothing but the beauty in them, I could see they had been treated like delicate butterflies, nurtured until their chrysalis set them free with sturdy wings. They would spend their lives flitting from flower to flower on the tip of the wind, confident and at ease.

I was angry and jealous of them.

My father broke my chrysalis shell before my wings had a chance to properly develop. I could choose my path, yes, but my path on the ground looked very different from my counterparts in the air.

How does a stunted caterpillar meet the butterfly where they are? If I was to have wings, I would have to build them myself. If I wanted to see the world from the other girls' perspectives, I would have to clamber, with bloody fingernails and sweaty skin, to their level.

A friend once said that bad parents can make good examples. He was right.

I would build my wings, and in the process, I would guard my daughter's chrysalis so she could grow hers. Even if I never made it into the air, God help me, my daughter would.

Chapter 7
Waiting for Batman

When I was a kid, I idolized my brother. Being four years older than me and the only constant male figure in my life, he often filled the void my father left behind. As adults, his passion for being a better parent than our father was rivaled only by my own. It was our invisible bond.

As children, we bonded through nature. We explored the woods behind our house with wonder, as all adventurous explorers would. We crept through the crackling branches and lush grass searching for aliens and treasure. Sometimes, rather than looking for excitement, we just wanted to escape the house into the silence of the countryside where trees cast cool shadows and underbrush quieted our footsteps.

In our more energetic moods, we would rush down the hill to the creek and pull crawdads out from the noisy stream while keeping a cautious eye out for snakes. We'd get dirty from the mud and wet from the stream, and it was all okay. But if his friend down the lane would show up on his three-wheeler, my brother would run to get his. I'd beg him to take me too. When he let me come along, the warm wind on my wet hair felt like childhood. Our childhood.

At times, I had hoped that maybe Savannah would have a sibling. Someone she could traipse through life with, who would know all her secrets, who would be the only other person on Earth who understood what it meant to be part of our family. But I never had another child. So instead, I took Savannah on walks, threw parties so she could make friends, and gave her my time and effort. It was not the same, of course, but it was still special. My daughter and I knew each other better than anyone else knew us.

And I knew my brother better than anyone else.

In our childhood, the brother I knew was on fire most of the time. He was either on fire, starting fires, or somehow in the middle of a fire. If someone yelled, "Fire!" I started looking for my brother. We had smoke detectors and fire extinguishers, and our mom made rules about matches. At one point, there was a rule about magnifying glasses and sunbeams. Lighters were not permitted, and there were several access points for water. I knew how to escape the house in case of a fire. Not because anyone told me how but because I had a desire to live.

This knowledge was put into practice when my brother and I were at home playing upstairs alone one day. I walked in his room and saw him with his G.I. Joes in the closet. He also had a forbidden match in his hand.

"You're not allowed to have those."

"Go away, dummy!"

"I'm telling Mom." As I went to tattle, something didn't smell right.

That's about the time my mom came tearing up the stairs screaming, "What did you do?"

The smoke began to billow from his room as the two of them put out the fire in his closet. My mom gave him hell for "damn near burning down the house with your little sister in it."

When I went in to see what I had escaped, I choked a little on the smoky air as I looked in the closet. A ten-inch circle of crisped, formerly blue carpet surrounded the blackened G.I. Joe soldiers in the center. He'd melted their faces off and damn near killed us. Even though he got beat for it, I'm pretty sure he was proud of that.

He was also proud of his work on my Barbie dolls. On an almost monthly basis their heads would go missing. When I finally found them, the hair was burned off and their faces were melted. I'd say he was a serial killer, but he took no satisfaction in the act itself. His satisfaction came when I stumbled on the crispy doll heads and started screaming as tears streamed down my face.

He also enjoyed grossing me out, and he did this often too. One time, when Mom assigned him the task of picking ticks off the dog, he figured out a way to rope me in to helping him. We lived in the country, so he wasn't just picking the ticks off but also killing them. So that's the scene I stumbled on when I walked into the garage.

"Hey, Steph, come here."
"Why?"

And it was always a cautious, "Why?" because there was never a pot of gold at the end of any rainbow with my brother. Something was always destroyed, and something was always melted. So, I inched toward him, noting the glass jar with fat ticks, the dog, the tweezers, and of course a lighter.

"You're not supposed to have that."

"Wanna see something cool?"

Since being cool was the going exchange rate for betraying Mom, I said, "Uh-huh." Smiling and standing right over the jar was my first mistake. Leaning in when he took the tweezers to the dog was my second mistake.

He yanked that fat, green tick off the dog and turned around with a grin. I had a moment—even at six years old—when I knew what was about to happen, but I had no power to stop the forces already in motion. He aimed that tick right at my head and squeezed until it exploded. Blood spattered my face, and I started to cry. He started to laugh. I got mad and punched him, and then he punched me back. I cried some more because he was four years older and stronger and I bruised easily.

"Watch!" he yelled.

Tears blurred my vision as I watched him light the ticks in the jar on fire. They started popping like Jiffy Pop. Although I felt bad for the ticks, I was also relieved to see them go. It was never a good day if I ran my fingers through my hair and found one of those things latched to my skull. So, I marveled at how they popped all over the place. This time, my brother laughed with me not at me. He took great pride in making me smile. That made him the happiest of all.

This was the same big brother who used to dress up like the caped crusader and jump off my grandparent's fireplace yelling, "Batman!" As a baby, I would scream with delight as he ran around the room. My mom said I was the most serious infant she'd ever seen, and the only person who could crack me up was my big brother.

"It was his mission," she said. "He would always find ways to make you laugh."

The day he left for the military my laughter went with him. My mother was remarried. My brother was growing up. And I was the final Musketeer, standing alone, waiting for Batman.

As I got older, I found myself loving fireworks and fiery explosions in the movies. The more, the better. That's probably why I like the *John Wick*, *Die Hard*, and *Lethal Weapon* series so much. Everything is always on fire, and that reminds me of my brother, who always makes me laugh. The same little boy who burned my Barbie heads is also the grown man who protected me from the bad guys, wrote me letters while in the Army, helped me move one thousand times, gave me rent money when I was a single mother, and never skipped a birthday. He will always come if I light the sky with the Bat signal.

As brothers go, he's a great one. I love his mischievousness and that he gets me into trouble. I, with my cautious sensibilities, am always drawn to my brother's fervor for life. He lives it with force, unafraid and open to its possibilities. He has many qualities I envy and emulate. And now, he brings those qualities into Savannah's life.

He and I may not have had a father around, but we had each other. And in the hardest times of my life, he was there for me and Savannah, always acting as a positive example of how men can and should be supportive of the women in their lives. And for that, I am grateful.

Chapter 8
Under the Influence of Angels

I was at a career crossroads. I had left journalism for a corporate job that paid more money, which was a good choice. But after a couple years, I was struggling in a role that didn't fit me and I was miserable. It left me with the question: Should I stay in the corporate job of technical writing or jump back to journalism?

That was the thought running through my head when I was crammed in the VIP section of the Memorial Tournament at a packed and sweaty after-party.

"Drink?" my friend asked as she handed me a glass of wine.

I smiled as I sipped the sweet beverage among the crowd of diamond-wearing, label-showing, upper-class crust that strolled around me. They were nice enough, but it wasn't a place I felt terribly comfortable, wearing my second-hand clothing and worn-out shoes.

I eyed each person my friends spoke with, keeping quiet while I observed the people around me. The pleasantries were lovely, but I slipped into my own private thoughts about where I was at in my career and what the hell should I do next? I was torn. The choice had become more pressing over the last year and certainly within the last few weeks as I started to feel some depression at my current gig.

"Steph!"

I snapped to attention as my friends grabbed my arm. They started to pull me with them, but a sudden and surprising wave of people broke us apart. My friends were engulfed quickly in a tidal wave of flashy smiles as I was pulled back toward the place I had been. My eyes darted through the crowd, but they had seemingly disappeared.

"Stephanie?"

The kind male voice came from behind me. I turned to see a man I had never met before, who didn't seem like he fit in at this party either. The party was noisy, but the space between us was eerily quiet as though someone had pressed a localized mute button. Warmth emanated from him.

"Yes?"

"Enjoying the event?"

I eyed him for a moment, searching my mind for how I knew him, but nothing was surfacing. He had no one with him. His hands were in the pockets of his clean suit, and he made no reference to knowing me as a journalist or otherwise. He was just kind, and that was all.

Seeing my hesitation, he smiled. "So, what do you do?"

I half-laughed with a shrug and looked down at the glass in my hand.

As I started to answer, he interrupted politely and said, "You should be a writer."

71

"I'm sorry?" My head snapped up. "What did you . . ."

"Stephanie!"

I turned around to see who was calling my name as my friends reappeared out of nowhere and rushed up me.

"Oh, I was just talking to . . ." I turned back, but he was gone. Vanished. Thin air, the whole thing.

"Who were you talking to?" my friend asked as she looked around.

"He was right here."

"Let's go grab a drink." She pulled me in yet another direction.

I searched the crowd frantically for the rest of the evening, turning every corner, looking behind every wall, and opening every door. I never saw him again.

I had heard and read divine stories about angels on earth interacting with people at key moments in life. Or perhaps a higher power would motivate someone on Earth to act on their behalf, and that was also considered the touch of an angel. (I lean towards this theory.) In this case, I didn't initially accept that my interaction with the man was either of those options. Since my journalism brain was hard-wired to see the facts, I tried to find a reasonable explanation of the event. He knew me from the media, but I didn't know him. (It's a common occurrence). He had to run to the bathroom and then hurry home. (He didn't vanish). Or maybe he guessed what I was thinking. (It could happen).

But ultimately, the situation felt a touch too unusual and too personal. And it came at such a serendipitous moment that it was hard to dismiss. So, I stopped looking for facts and accepted the possibility that the man had been acting under the influence of an angel. It was the first of many UIA (Under the Influence of Angels) experiences I had while raising Savannah that kept us going. It was like a safety net keeping us alive, and I recognized its power.

The next UIA event came about two years later. I had a two thousand dollar dental bill that I had paid down to six hundred dollars over two years. One day, the receptionist I always worked with called me out of the blue.

"Stephanie. You won't believe what just happened."

She told me that a man, who wanted to remain anonymous, had come into the office the day before. This kind, gentle man told the front desk that he had recently inherited a few thousand dollars. He initially didn't know what to do with it, but then he was suddenly overwhelmed with a feeling to go to their office. (I call this moment of overwhelming inspiration "angel intoxication.") He told her staff to select three patients who really needed the help and pay off their accounts.

She said, "We applied six hundred dollars to your account. Your bill is paid off."

I was speechless. And relieved. I said a big thank you to the divine powers that be because having people around who were drunk on angel power was the kind of thing Savannah and I needed to make it.

Only a few months later, it happened again. My car broke down and had to be towed to the dealership where I knew the price tag would be hefty. So, I desperately pleaded with the man who was inspecting my car to call me before doing any work because I was a single mom on a strict budget with no warranty. He agreed.

The day turned into the night then into morning. I chewed my fingernails to the skin and tossed all night long. I got no sleep and drank two cups of coffee to wake up. What on Earth would I do? How would I pay for this? I walked to my apartment window and stared out on the street as the tears stung my eyes. How could I swing this? That's when the phone rang.

"Hello?"

"Stephanie?" the mechanic said.

"Yes?" I said, as I held my breath.

"Well, here's the story."

He explained how he came up with the $1,500 estimate. But before he called me, he did a quick check of any warranties I may have had despite me saying I had none.

"Your car was under warranty," he said.

He said that my stepfather had purchased an extended warranty a year before. (This was a warranty my stepdad had no recollection of purchasing, that never went to his house, and that I wasn't aware of.) The warranty covered all the work he had done, including the tow. And he had fixed a couple cosmetic issues on my car, free of charge.

So, my bill was zero.

"I was raised by a single mother," he said, "and I know how hard it can be."

That guy was for sure divinely drunk. I don't know what angel juice he'd been sipping on that morning, but halleluiah and praise be and all the glory. Write that man a ticket for UIA intoxication because I believe!

Miracles, moments of assumed coincidence, and times when you swear someone or something (depending on your beliefs) was watching over you may mean someone or something was. When I was the person called upon to provide a miracle, I listened to that voice and got drunk on angel power too. UIAs are for everyone by everyone here on Earth. We don't always know what someone is going through, but if we tune in to that angel frequency and are open to divine influence, then we can help in life changing ways. This is what it means to be under the influence of an angel and to be the miracle someone else needs.

When I paid attention to the moments in my life that seemed divine, I found the right path. In this case, the Memorial Tournament guy's drive-by UIA led me back to writing. I knew I needed to go back to journalism. And I did. With a bang.

Chapter 9
A Constellation of North Stars

I went back to journalism and became a writer for *The Other Paper*, the alternative weekly in Columbus, Ohio. I was happy to be there because my male editor had an alternative view on childcare that I'd never seen in my professional life just yet. He allowed me to leave mid-afternoon, pick up my daughter, and bring her back to the office with me so I could finish working.

He affectionately called Savannah our paper's team mascot. All of my coworkers knew her and often brought her candy. Once she was a cover girl for one of our company's community newspapers. With the exception of that one time when she erased all the sales team's monthly numbers from their white board—she said she was cleaning—it was a perfect set-up, and I was grateful.

My editor told me he had daughters, and he was doing what he would want someone else to do for his daughters. Fathers of daughters, I'd noticed, turned out to be excellent managers for women and single mothers. Plus, he just had a good heart for equality across the board. And I appreciated the example he set.

The Other Paper is also where I met Genevieve, one of the best people I've ever known. I don't know why she always called me "La Steph," but I loved the nickname. She also was a single mother and a passionate writer.

On the night Barack Obama won the U.S. presidential election in 2008, Genevieve and I were supposed to be inside the Franklin County Democratic headquarters. But we couldn't get in. The press passes in our hands, which had opened nearly every door in the city to us, were suddenly not opening anything.

"We're getting in," I said.

"Damn straight," she said.

We were not going to miss our opportunity to cover what was, by all standards, a historic election night. But because history was being made, everyone wanted to be at the hottest party in Columbus, which was being held at a downtown hotel. Guests in attendance had already started partying when the projections leaned towards Obama. Most of the attendees were pleasantly pickled, and the celebration was fast approaching fire code overcrowding, so the door police were doing their jobs and limiting who got in.

But we had deadlines to meet, so we had to get creative. Since going door-to-door and simply explaining our situation did not work, we regrouped. We decided that committing a crime in plain sight (although it was hardly a crime since we had our passes to be there), while sweet talking the door police and eventually the guards would likely work.

First Genevieve went up and started talking to the policeman. When someone else came up to talk to him, she used the distraction to sneak through the door. I waited until she was safely inside, and then I made my move. The next person who came up to ask a question and divert his attention allowed me to slip by as well. We met in the lobby and pretended like we were supposed to be there—wait, we were— before deciding our next move.

"We only have one more guard to get past," she said.

We turned to look at the security guard in front of the stairs leading up to the room where the party was now in full swing. The thumping music and joyous yells called to us. So, we put on our lip gloss, fluffed up our girls, and headed over with a smile. It only took a few minutes to work our magic before the security guard let us up.

It ended up being a great story in the paper, but more than that, I knew I had a great friend.

It's not every day a girl finds a partner in crime to sneak into the best political after-party on a historic election night. Or to talk single motherhood over cocktails. Or to cry on a shoulder that understood. She was a good friend. A great friend. My best friend. She listened to me talk while I cried out my broken heart, and I did the same for her. In between all that, our mighty little team wrote some of the best, most controversial news you could get in Columbus. The years spent at that paper were some of the most exquisite I'd ever known for many reasons, but certainly one of them was Genevieve.

I've always had friends who were willing to break the rules, challenge the norms, and push against society's version of what a woman should be. There was Ms. Strawberry, who helped me throw a high school party that rocked everyone's world. Then my college girls, who even after graduating, were always willing to drink wine, travel, and define womanhood on their own terms.

Ms. Massillon, who was my friend in dating and sex, would always encourage me to have the best, safest fun I could on my dates. She always said, "After all, we could, and should, have the same fun as men if we want to on our terms." Ms. Navarre, a single mother herself at one time, helped me with necessities when I found myself choosing between gas, food, or rent. And Ms. Elementary, who helped me with childcare so I could work.

Ms. Gamer, with her sass and snark, encouraged me to write provocative news pieces. She expected my voice to be as powerful as any reporter out there regardless of gender. There were my girl's night out ladies and their beautiful, accepting spirits. And Ms. Riverside, Ms. Sparkle, and Ms. Cat Attack, who were always ready to offer support to each other in the best and worst times of being a woman in this world.

I've also had many aunties, across multiple families, with their spirited notion of the male-female dynamic. Like me, they loved men, wanted marriage, and ran great households. But, like me, they weren't about to give up their independence, their right to speak, their right to make their own choices, or any other rights in order to please a man. I carried great pride in the gumption of the women in my family. The experience of packing up a female family member in the middle of the night and moving her to safety impressed upon me my right to survive and thrive in this world. As did watching several aunties save up their own money to buy real estate so they could have their own financial assets.

Sadly, my beautiful and loving Auntie Arizona was taken from us too soon. She died quickly from breast cancer, but her spirit always remained. She loved fiercely and completely, raising her daughters to be equally fierce. And my stepsister, Ms. Scrabble, who also passed away from cancer. She fought for her life with such grace, humility, and strength that it redefined for me what it meant to be a female warrior.

And, of course, there was Genevieve, who was a combination of all these women, whip smart, fierce, and unapologetic.

These friendships were a reminder of the value of female relationships and their importance to me. Every woman I called a friend was not only a source of comfort in my highs and lows but each was also my north star. I had found myself always navigating a world that was opposed, on many levels, to me having agency and choices in my life for the mere fact that I was a woman. And not just a woman, but a strong, opinionated one.

Because of that, it became necessary to find my tribe of female friends who had gumption by the bucketful. My female friends owned their voices and made no apologies for them. Whether they were stay-at-home moms, business owners, writers, social media experts, college educated or not they were first and foremost strong women with good hearts. They each believed in their core that they should be afforded the same rights and privileges as men and anything less than that was unacceptable.

That belief was an invisible bridge we all walked on. It was our united pathway forward. But because we lived in a society that said women were inferior, there was also a competitiveness among us. This competition was born of limited partners, limited job opportunities, and limited access. We were pitted daily against each other for love, money, power, and security. And because women had to fight so hard to earn these things, when one finally got to the top, she had to protect her post.

This had always been true for me because I wanted to rule whatever role I was in. But not everyone was open to that kind of energy from a female.

My ability to compete was also complicated by the fact I was overweight for most of my life. Thin, attractive women often used their sexual appeal to move ahead of rivals. I used my smarts. Over time, I started to feel that this approach was demeaning to both types of women. Beautiful women could be smart; overweight women could be sexy. And why did we have to use any wiles to move up the ladder at all? The best person for the job should get the role, right? And if a woman wants to rule it all, why shouldn't she?

But life does not work that way, of course. Inevitably, women would see each other as competition to getting what they wanted and needed. And inevitably, we would play to men however we could for our security because they held the key to our futures. As the award-winning TV show *Orange is the New Black* taught us when a prison guard impregnated a prisoner—a prisoner (women) cannot consent to her captor (men with power). Consent implies freedom of choice, and for many women, there is no such thing in this world. So, we use whatever wiles we have to get what we need, because choice for most women is an illusion.

I didn't want my gender or my weight to define my success anymore. And I certainly didn't want it to define my female friendships. The more I became aware of this dynamic, the more realizations about my body and its impact on my life began to emerge.

Chapter 10
Victoria's Secret Lie

When I was a teenager, Victoria's Secret didn't carry their youth line Pink. But even if they had, my conservative mother would never have let me wear the clothing. Not that I would have fit in it if she had. I was as big as a full-grown adult in the eighth grade at five foot ten and 170 pounds, which made me an athlete but not so much a girlfriend. Not even my big, teased brown hair and braces stopped new students from asking me what classes I taught.

Then I blew up into a 250-pound twenty-something who hit 318 pounds after my daughter was born. Nothing in any of the then-popular stores fit my body. Even Lane Bryant had capped out on me. The first day I was able to buy a normal pair of jeans from Old Navy was one of the best days in my weight loss life.

I expected my first time buying Victoria's Secret lingerie at age thirty-four to feel the same. For years I had watched teeny, tiny women walk out of that store with teeny, tiny bags that held teeny, tiny things that I could only imagine fitting into. The moment I knew their clothes would fit was sweeter than all the desserts I had given up since I started my weight loss journey. I was down 160 pounds to 160 pounds. I had literally lost half of myself.

But the moment I stumbled into the jungle of teeny, tiny things and saw those exotic XS/S creatures eyeing my M/L five-foot ten frame from behind racks of tiny panties with tiny strings, I realized the competition I was up against.

Holy shit! These were the girls that the guys I had dated—or wanted to date—ended up with.

"Oh my God," I said to myself as they swarmed like tiny airplanes around my King Kong physique. My jaw dropped. I had told myself that these girls didn't really exist because I had only seen them in ads and on posters. After all, they hadn't existed in my world of Lane Bryant or the Ben and Jerry's aisle at Giant Eagle. But they did exist here. They were like a group of mythological sirens lounging around in warm, misty springs.

"Can I help you find something?" a petite brunette asked as she moved toward me like a panther from behind a rack of fantasies. She smelled like expensive perfume.

Wal-Mart doesn't sell that scent.

I tucked my home-kit bleached hair behind my ear and smoothed down my second-hand clothes. I stared at the glossy, brown hair cascading around her chest and knew the seductive charm she held over men. The opposite sex wanted nothing more than the touch of silk sheets mixed with her sweet, uncomplicated smell of vanilla.

"No, I'm fine, thanks." I headed in the opposite direction of her petite stare. I smelled a few perfumes, looked at a few lip glosses, and waded through the naughty corset and panty sets before

85

picking up a few full-coverage items and heading to the dressing room.

My sagging frame was met at the dressing room door by a perky five-foot two blonde dressed in black heels, a tight skirt, and what I guessed were thigh highs stockings and a push-up bra.

Sweet Lord, they're everywhere!

I had stared at their flat bellies on the covers of *Maxim* and *Playboy* and their beach body critiques in *US Weekly* and *In Touch*. They sashayed across my TV screen during the swimsuit competition in the Miss America pageant. They were the hot girls on the workout tapes.

Touching my sagging belly through my shirt, I felt weary of the gap that, after all this time and weight loss and hard work, still existed between them and me. They represented the lie the fitness industry and the beauty industry and the fashion industry had told me. I felt duped.

"I'll take those for you," said the perky blonde with perfectly manicured eyebrows.

Staring at her backside, I sighed as she placed my mishmash of items on the hook. Was she judging me as she hung my unmentionables? I'm sure my frame looked small enough to slide these lacy numbers on my body. Could she see the lump of loose skin protruding just above my belly button? It was one of many lumps of loose skin from weight loss.

"If you need a different size, just push this button and I'll come help." She smiled sweetly as she tossed her blonde hair and closed the door behind her. Men loved women like her. They loved that they were small and light, tiny and protectable. I knew this because some of my most beloved girlfriends were tiny.

Tiny women lived charmed lives. Even when they met with misfortune, that simply added to their charm. They're like cute, little kittens. And people love to cuddle kittens. When bad things happen to hot, tiny women, society shrieks in a collective gasp, "We can't lose the tiny ones!" They are society's trophies, so they must be protected at all costs.

One of my best friends in college was tiny. During that time, I was crushing on a guy who had blue eyes and was quiet in a very James Dean-like way. He was a guitar player with a deep soul, and I wanted to be close to him. But the closer he got to me, the closer he wanted to get to her. He used to ask me about her all the time. She was perfectly lovely at five foot two with her easy laugh, taut stomach, and cropped brunette hair. She once wrapped that petite frame in black, leather pants for a party that my college guitar player went to.

Shortly after that on the way to a fraternity party, my guitar-playing crush again asked about her and if she would be around. I yelled from the backseat, "Stop asking me about her!" He glanced sideways at his friend and made an oops face. He never asked me about her again, but the resentment was firmly planted in my psyche. She wasn't just my friend anymore; she was my adversary. I could love her, but only so far as it didn't hurt me.

I re-learned what it meant to be invisible that night.

In her book *Men Explain Things to Me*, Rebecca Solnit talks about the obliteration of women throughout history by making them invisible. Sometimes this was done by denying them rights, by keeping them silent through threats and violence, or even removing them from family trees. She added that in some societies, forcing women to wear veils literally made them disappear. I would also argue that weight is like a cloak of invisibility. Women who are overweight are ignored, unnoticed, and otherwise erased from society's view.

I felt invisible. And every bad gene I had been dealt was spilling out of me. My parents, of course, did not intend to pass on the worst of themselves to me—no parent does. It was the luck of the draw. My body was the result of genetic roulette rolling from generation to generation and nothing more. There was nothing poetic about recessive genes making my eyes blue or dominant genes making my hair brown. Or ancestral Irish traits making my skin pale and freckled. Or my parents passing on the large, German-woman hips to me. It was science.

And yet, I had paid dearly for science from very early on. Paid for my large hips and chubby genes as though I had custom-ordered them off the menu. Being routinely punished for something I had no control over was baffling. And others being so richly rewarded for things they had no control over was equally mystifying. Gisele Bundchen is not Gisele Bundchen without her parents' good genes. But she is praised and paid and paraded as though her bone structure and metabolism were her own doing. As if any of those models were responsible for their genes. What they do after they're born matters of course—many models work out, I'm aware—but where they begin is so different from most women that they're starting with an advantage that's never acknowledged.

I stood in the changing room and slowly reached for the first of my confections and began the unmerciful punishment of dragging fat-squishing garments up and down what felt like my giant, bloated body. The half corsets were lovely until my hands went above my head and the loose skin flipped out. The panty sets created multiple problems: first, if the panties clung even a little bit to my loose skin, the elasticity of the band would force the skin to flop out over the panty line like a drooping mess; second, the matching crop-corset top combined with that hanging elastic skin, created a roll of loose skin below its edges that circled my entire waist; and third, if any of

89

those pieces had a push-up bra, it would cause my breasts to wrinkle like crepe paper.

Sweat beads gathered on my angry brow.

I'm supposed to be tiny by now!

One hundred sixty pounds gone and still I wasn't there. Pouring my loose, unmanageable skin into stiff clothes in a cramped space was not what I had expected from this experience. I stared into Victoria's Secret mirror at what had become a hollow reflection. I had worked as hard as anyone to have the same body, but I still fell short.

Tired and emotionally spent, I walked to the shiny black counter and waited for the petite blonde to ring up the best-I-could-find-for-my-body corset.

"That'll be one hundred ten dollars." She smiled with white teeth as she cocked her head to the side.

I smiled back with my whitened, half-fake smile as I slowly reached for my bank card and did some math in my head.

Maybe I can go without this.

An image of the bills on my table loomed in my mind. Just then, a tiny woman zoomed past me, and someone's boyfriend did a double take of her impossibly adorable figure.

"You take Visa?" I asked as I handed her my card. She smiled and I was struck by how pearly her teeth really were. Did she pay for that with her own money, or did some man pay for it?

"Credit or debit?"

"Debit."

"All right, if you could just sign here," she said, handing me the receipt.

I probably just paid for her to get even better looking.

"Thank you." I headed for the entrance where the petite brunette waited in her cloud of vanilla-scented sex appeal.

"Have a good day," she said with that cleverly raised eyebrow of hers.

"You too," I said as I walked out.

I flipped the front of that Victoria's Secret bag toward every man I passed searching for any takers who might want to pay for my teeth to be whitened one day. I got a few looks. They were flirting with me as though I had no scars, as though my body wasn't destroyed, as though my breasts and my stomach were normal. There would be nowhere for me and my scars to hide once I was naked. Once the Victoria's Secret lie came off.

The duplicitous life I was leading was exhausting. I didn't know how to reconcile the truth of who I was (strong and capable) with the lie I had to tell (sexy and a plaything). The truth was a damning realization of both how far I'd come and how far I'd fallen behind all at the same time. I'd lost all this weight to find some semblance of who I was. When I got to the top of the mountain, I'd found only another mountain to climb. And another. And another. My own body had turned on me. Once the

91

clothes came off, who would love someone with so many scars?

I was too embarrassed of my body to reconcile its marred scars with the strength it had taken me to make them. I could not accept my body and soul as one, no matter how hard I tried. I'd thought becoming thinner would bring those two worlds together, change me, and change the way men thought of me. Finding out that nothing had changed was devastating. I just wanted to be loved, but it seemed like nothing I did could get me to that place. Or even a place where I could love myself.

And, worse, I wasn't sure who would pay more for that brokenness—me or Savannah?

Chapter 11
Fat Belly Wrecked

The look in his dark brown eyes was smoldering. The richness of their color drew me in immediately as his smile melted into a mischievous grin.

"Can I get your number?" asked Mr. Athlete. His confidence was a force of nature. He was arrogant and charming, alluring in every bad way my girlfriends had warned me about.

I was completely attracted to him.

Pausing, I steadied myself, wondering if this was a good idea or not. He just raised an eyebrow and waited patiently. My hesitancy was a brief obstacle he shooed away with the flick of his wrist as he pulled out his phone. To him, getting my number was inevitable.

"Sure." I shrugged as I listed off my number and watched him skillfully enter it into his contacts, a move he'd done a million times before.

"Thanks." He smiled as he swaggered away.

A nervous laugh escaped my lips. I was a rookie in this world of athletes or big businessmen or high-ranking officials who were suddenly interested in sleeping with me. Now weighing 150 pounds at five-foot-ten with blonde hair and blue eyes, I caught the attention of a new category of men previously beyond my reach. These were trophy wife men.

As a member of that elite club, Mr. Athlete was rewarding me for a job well done with the simple act of asking for my number. It felt good to be seen by him, to be objectified by him. His gaze was the thing that made me feel like a sexual being. By the standards I had grown up with, this was the only way for a woman to feel like a woman, right? So, I did.

He was my human measuring stick. In fact, men had been my human measuring sticks since that day I stumbled upon my father's dirty magazines. Somewhere inside me was a primal urge to look like those women. Not just because men thought they were beautiful but because I did too. And not because they sold sex but because they sold the notion of perfection.

As I chased that perfection, I gauged my beauty and value by how seriously men responded to me as I lost weight. Their actions told me whether I was pretty or fat. If I was asked on a legitimate date in public and my dinner was paid for, I knew I was pretty. If I was asked to sleep with them in the backseat without anyone knowing, I was fat.

That was the way Mr. High School, a star athlete who was hot and unattainable, told me I was fat. One fateful fall evening, he called me to play tennis. My sixteen-year-old brain immediately started firing questions off: Was this the start of something? Did he *like* like me? Or did he make a mistake and call the wrong girl? I was the Monica of my high school. I'd never been kissed or asked on a date. I'd never been asked to dance at a school dance. So, Mr. High School accidentally dialing the wrong number was a distinct possibility.

I took care with my appearance, making sure my hair was teased as high it could be and my blue eyeliner was done just right. My friendship bracelets were properly lined up on my wrist, and my braces were free of debris. I spot-concealed my acne and sprayed a little of Debbie Gibson's Electric Youth perfume on my wrists to complete the package.

I arrived at the tennis courts that night looking pretty or at least as pretty as I could at sixteen years old with acne and braces. I had my tennis racket in hand and my nerve built up. I was finally going to do something real with one of the popular boys in high school.

"Let's talk for a second." He looked me over as I got out of my car. "Hop in my van."

My braces were vibrating with excitement. *He actually wants to talk! Is he going to ask me on a date?*

"So . . ." he said, leaning forward and touching my leg. "You wanna give me a blow job?"

"Uh . . ."

"Come on," he said as his hand slid up my thigh.

"No!" I jumped out of his van, nearly falling onto the pavement, then ran to my car and sped off.

That "no" was the first of many to a long line of secret suitors, who only liked me in private because dating the fat girl was taboo. To be clear, it was never that they didn't find me attractive—they most certainly did. Being fat didn't matter to them because they still thought I had a pretty face. Plus, I was semi-popular. (Think of the group of kids who sat in the middle of the high school hierarchy and were friends with almost everyone). And I was a middle tier athlete. No, their issue was what other people would think about them liking the fat girl.

Take, for example, Mr. Country. He was a boy in my high school who really liked me. He was sweet, funny, good-looking, and also a middle tier athlete. He had told my friend he was going to ask me out. I was so excited. It would have been my first date in high school and with someone I really liked. He was the perfect counterweight to Mr. High School. Day after day, I waited for the moment to arrive. I waited. And waited. And waited. The weekend came and went. No date.

My friend went to him on Monday to find out why he didn't ask me out. Apparently, when he told his friends about his plans, they made fun of him for being into the fat girl. The next weekend, he went out with a cheerleader.

Both boys were secret suitors. Guys who privately like the girls they're not supposed to while parading around the girls they are supposed to like. Secret suitors are too weak to stand up to their critics about how they really feel.

But other men restored my hope that there were males in this world who would not only stand up to societal norms but also do it in the name of love and friendship and basic human dignity. Mr. Husband, of course, was my first romance. He loved me no matter what—God love him for that—at any weight. And he always showed it publicly with the diamond ring and everything.

There was also Mr. College. Ah, Mr. College. He had the brightest blue eyes I'd ever seen, and he had a crush on me. On Valentine's Day of my sophomore year, the school held a fundraiser where students bought flowers for each other. But because of a snow storm, they couldn't finish delivering the floral surprises. Once he found out his package wasn't going to be delivered, Mr. College went out and got the twelve carnations he'd bought, walked across campus in snow that was three feet deep, and delivered them to me in person at ten o'clock at night. Talk about restoring faith in men.

And then there was Mr. Politico, whom I met through my work at *The Other Paper*. He and I were both reporters, but he covered politics while I covered general news, crime, and sports. We became friends because of a Facebook friend-request blackmail situation.

Mr. Politico, employed by a local rival paper, would only accept my coworker's Facebook friend request if she—disliked by his editors because she also covered politics—would get me to accept his friend request. The deal was done, and we all celebrated with drinks at happy hour.

As soon as we met in real life, we were instant friends. He was handsome and insanely intelligent. An attraction developed and we dated briefly before he moved to another state for work. Despite his move, we always kept each other close, which was different than much of the dating I'd been doing.

I had kept men at arm's length since I was assaulted all those years ago. I would date them and sleep with them when Savannah was gone. When she returned, I returned to my life as Mom and left the thought of men behind. A clear delineation existed between me, as a single woman dating, and me, as a mother protecting my daughter.

Men, of course, had a hard time understanding this dichotomy. Single mothers have a much different dating world than single women with no children.

"You can't just *date* a single mother," I said to one male friend at a bar. We were playing pool, and I was winning. "When you add a child to the equation, there's an additional level of care that you guys have to incorporate into your game."

"Yeah, I don't want to deal with that," he replied. "Too much drama. Hit it and quit it."

"You're a dick," I said. He laughed. To make my point, I threw out Cuba Gooding Jr.'s line from *Jerry Maguire*. "A real man wouldn't shoplift the pootie from a single mother."

But whether I was fat or thin, secret or public, they all still tried. Except Mr. Politico. He remained one of my best friends. After he moved, he sent me a care package with a vintage Def Leppard T-shirt, a small vial of sweet-smelling perfume, and a few other trinkets. I sent him Buckeyes—the candy— straight from the heart of Columbus, postcards from a little German Village bookstore, and a mix CD. Mr. Politico was my dating guru, too. And he was highly opposed to this tryst with Mr. Athlete.

I told him, "I know it's a fling. That's why I want to do it."

"Not a good idea," he said. This was his stance on Mr. Athlete or any guy that wouldn't take me seriously because Mr. Politico did take me seriously, at any weight, at any time, and especially when I needed him. He and Mr. Husband were the exceptions to the societal rule about not only who I should be attracted to but also who should be attracted to me.

Despite his sound advice, however, I jumped in anyway. I had to see for myself even though Genevieve agreed with Mr. Politico. Normally, she wanted me to have great sex without strings. Women like string-free sex as much as men and are often better for it. It gives women the opportunity to learn their sexual preferences, what gets them off, and how to have some fun without it having to mean

99

everything. But this time, she was concerned about my reasons for doing it with Mr. Athlete, which may not have been about good sex but rather my emotional state of mind about my body.

"I think you seek out people who criticize you," she quipped. "And then you conquer that person and their criticism to prove something that you don't need to prove."

She wasn't wrong. The same way an abused child seeks out the familiarity of abuse, I was seeking out the familiar pain of the secret suitor to see if anything had changed. Because the truth was, if Mr. Athlete and I had traversed the same hallways as teenagers, he never would have laid a finger on me. He would have breezed by me without a thought, been nice to me when he wanted to ask out one of my thin friends, and made fun of me when my back was turned. In short, he would have been a secret suitor.

But that criticism and body shaming wasn't just from men, secret suitors, or Mr. Athlete. It was women too. And mean, teenage girls who yelled, "That fat lady shouldn't be wearing a bikini," right in front of my young daughter. This was after I'd lost about 110 pounds and was proud of everything I'd accomplished.

Savannah's eyes immediately filled with tears as she watched them laugh at me, feeling helpless to do or say anything. "Mom, those girls said that about you." Tears started to overflow her big, blue eyes.

"It's okay, Savannah. I'm proud of what I've done. They just don't know better."

She looked uncertain and a little bit protective, but she went back to building a sandcastle. I just kept reading my magazine. After a few minutes, I asked my mom to watch her, then I went to a bathroom stall and cried.

I'm sure those painful experiences were the reason I told my daughter, at eight years old, that her stomach was too chubby, and she needed to stop eating so much candy.

"You're going to get fat." I slammed down the laundry basket. I didn't notice her start to cry until I turned to put the clothes away.

"I just mean that loving yourself is great, but being fat makes everything harder." I tried to erase those horrible, terrible words, but I couldn't. And somewhere inside, I didn't want to. Whatever issues my daughter would battle in her lifetime, I didn't want being fat to be one of them. Being overweight was the transformative aspect of my entire life. And now, the leftover skin following weight loss was equally transformative.

When I showed my friends the scars that extreme weight loss left behind, they would cringe in disgust and immediately ask, "Can you have plastic surgery?" Because it is human nature to be repulsed and appalled by those things which we associate with pain, discomfort, and abnormality. It's like watching a movie and feeling so embarrassed for an actor who's making an ass of themself that you must look away. That's how my friends looked at me.

I never wanted Savannah's friends to look at her that way.

"One fruit, one vegetable, one po-tein," she said as she carefully packed her lunch for school.

"Protein, with an r." I smiled at her as she dropped in her tuna pack. "Make sure you go out on the playground and run around. Get some exercise."

"Okay, Mommy."

A few months later, she and I were getting ready to go swimming, and I found her favorite two-piece swimsuit in the drawer.

"Savannah?" I called out as I held it up.

She came out from the bathroom in a one-piece Speedo my mother had gotten her.

"Why aren't you wearing this one?" I asked, knowing in my stomach why.

She looked down at her toes as though something terribly interesting was happening down there.

"Savannah?"

She hemmed and hawed even more, rocking back and forth.

"Savannah, it's fine, whatever your reason. I'm just curious."

She finally looked up at me, then pointed at her stomach. "Fat belly."

Dammit!

102

"Oh, Savannah, that's not what I meant."
My mind raced to find ways that I could re-arrange
those words and make them mean what they were
supposed to and not what they had. I had failed, as a
parent, to separate the concern of what I knew to be
true of the world from who I thought she was as a
person and how I viewed her as a child.

"Honey, I love you no matter what." I
picked her up and squeezed her. "There is absolutely
nothing wrong with you. You're perfect."

After a few moments, I gave her a kiss on
the cheek and set her down. She looked up at me with
a smile.

"Wear whatever you feel good in, buddy.
Let's just go have fun together, okay?"

Her grin brightened as she grabbed all her
toys and headed for the door.

I never wanted my daughter to trade a piece
of her soul the same way I was about to with Mr.
Athlete. I knew when my clothes dropped in front of
him, he would change his mind. Not just about sex
with me, but about me as a human. Gone would be
the illusion, and ushered in would be the reality. I
wasn't fat anymore, but I had loose skin and scars
from losing the fat. And I would do anything to hide
that reality in exchange for one night of being the
tiny girl, the special one, the one who finally got to
be chosen.

I stared in the mirror and lifted the sagging
skin off my tummy.

There I am.

I eyed what my body would look like if a plastic surgeon excised that extra skin.

That's who I should have been all along.

I let go of the skin and turned away as it drooped back into place. I chose my outfit for the evening with Mr. Athlete: a black summer skirt that didn't cinch at the waist and a tank top that was fitted but still loose. I just wouldn't take my clothes off.

Helen Gurley Brown preached in her 1962 book, *Sex and the Single Girl*, a theology that is still true today about a woman's body and its value to society. Slim girls get the boys. "This shape business is important," she wrote of a single girl's figure, "if you're not going to take singleness lying down—except when you want to."

And it is a business, of sorts, especially in relationships. There is a give and take, supply and demand. In every society throughout history, the trophy wife (with her perfect figure and exquisite beauty) is a form of commerce. She's the only commodity that can't be placed on Wall Street's stock exchange.

You can tell very early on which girls will become the prized kept women and which ones won't. I knew at age eight and at age sixteen and at age twenty which woman I would be. And I hated it. No, I hated that the ideal even existed. I hated that being a woman meant that everything about me, all the thoughts and ideas and emotions and dreams and

104

skills were boiled down to the one thing that had any meaning in society: my size.

But now, I had a rendezvous with Mr. Athlete, and he was exactly the trophy I needed. I knew Genevieve and Mr. Politico couldn't understand that, but I did. So, after a few casual meet-ups, a couple phone calls, and several flirty texts, we planned a night together. I walked in through the unlocked front door and slipped off my sandals. I tip-toed up the stairs to his all-white bedroom where the night's basketball game was playing on his high-res television.

"Hey." He muted the game as his eyes met mine.

"Hey." I hoped he wouldn't see the anxiety in my eyes as I climbed in his bed.

I didn't know Mr. Athlete's favorite color or what he liked for dinner or how he took his coffee or if he even drank coffee. I didn't care and neither did he. I only knew that he was a proxy for every secret suitor who had ever made me feel less than. So, I relaxed and let him make me feel better.

With every move of his hips and look in his eyes, he erased my painful past. A kiss across my neck wiped away the dateless nights when I watched my friends go through boyfriend after boyfriend. His hands on my body wiped away the feelings of never being wanted and never being seen as sexual for years and years.

This was the first time I'd recognized sex as therapy. Like resin in a cracked windshield, I was healing almost immediately from the inside out every time he touched my body. Mr. Athlete changed me. My spine was straighter and stronger. My resolve to keep going strengthened. As a woman, I felt redeemed, somehow.

I also felt sick. The same way you feel when you eat too much dessert. In the moment, it's like delicious, "Nom, nom, nom." But an hour later, you're rubbing your belly like, "Why did I do that?"

I changed the way I looked, in part, to get a guy like Mr. Athlete. I got him. But not because of who I was. It was only because of the way I looked. And once I got it, I recognized that it was a double-edged sword I wasn't comfortable with.

Well, fuck.

Having lived both extremes of body weight, I'm certain that when a man makes any decision about a woman, he considers first and foremost her body and her looks. As a heavy woman, if I was given an opportunity, I was sure that I'd gotten it because I'd earned it. As a thin woman, I was never quite clear about why an opportunity existed for me. For the first time in my life, I began questioning the how and why of everything.

I'd heard the men in my life say, "Who cares how you got the opportunity. Just take it and do what you can with it." But as a woman living in a world where power and money were disproportionately controlled by men, I could tell that that my male friends and family members had clearly never had to put their bodies or looks on the line to get their basic needs met. And because of that, they could not understand that the how and why of it mattered. Or at least, it was starting to matter to me. And shouldn't it matter to all women?

I began to ask the question: Are women weaker for playing a man's game rather than playing by our own rules with our own power and money? Shouldn't we care that our bodies and looks are often the primary thing getting us through the door? Shouldn't a beautiful woman be concerned that her looks got her in, while a more qualified woman with perhaps more experience did not get in because she was less attractive?

As I started to contemplate the nuances of what it meant to be a working single mother in a professional world dominated by men—and the uncomfortable truths about bodies and looks associated with that world—I was offered an incredible opportunity. A hiring manager from the National Hockey League came knocking. And my questions were about to come to the forefront of my life.

Chapter 12
NHL vs. Savannah

I stared at my Twitter inbox and re-read the message.

"You may be a good fit for the NHL. You interested?"

A huge smile erupted across my face. This was a game-changing, once-in-a-lifetime opportunity in New York City, and it was sitting in my messages ready for the taking.

When I told my coworker, Genevieve, she said, "That's amazing! Savannah will love New York."

"I know! So exciting." I turned to my computer and finished reading the message.

"Come to New York for an interview," wrote the man I affectionately called Mr. NHL. He was a handsome guy, who was slightly older than me, had a penchant for rooftop drinks in the city, and an edgy sense of humor. He'd been following my coverage of the Columbus Blue Jackets for a while and saw a spark in me that he thought would translate to the league.

I had acclimated quickly to the world of ice hockey while covering the Jackets, winning a few writing awards and earning my place, so this opportunity felt like a natural next step. However, I knew he thought I was interesting beyond just my work, so it crossed my mind that perhaps this opportunity was a way to get closer to me. But because I knew he was a big gun for the NHL, I trusted that he had a responsibility to recruit qualified talent that could perform the work more than anything else.

"Yes, I'm interested," I wrote back. "Tell me more."

He was considering me for a digital marketing job, and my interview was in two weeks. I prepared a resume that included an analysis of the current NHL digital slate and how I would build upon it over the next year to grow the league's social standing and sent it to him.

The position was a step-up from the job I was currently doing and loving. While working at the Columbus alternative newspaper, *The Other Paper*, I also helped build their social media presence. Like everything in my life up to this point, when I was confronted with a challenge at work, I would listen, research, and teach myself what was necessary to excel at the job and get a promotion. So, when I asked my editor why we weren't covering the Jackets, he answered that nobody had picked up the beat when the guy who was doing it left. I asked to go to a game and was officially hooked, learning everything about the sport from blue lines to fisticuffs.

The sensory experience alone was amazing. The smell of cold would fill my nostrils the moment I entered the rink. The same way I could smell rain before a storm, I could close my eyes and inhale the crisp scent of ice before I was anywhere near the rink. The hiss of the players' skates cutting and digging and stopping and slicing across the ice was an addicting sound of sporty competitiveness I couldn't get anywhere else.

Hockey was like nothing anything I'd ever seen. It was brutal but beautiful. And now, I was being offered a chance to work within the hallowed halls of the organization that brought the game to life. If I got hired, I would be an integral part of telling the league's story through social and digital media.

Since my beloved industry of print journalism was dying, thanks to the digital revolution, I knew that if I wanted to have a job, I had to change with the times. So, my bags were packed. The car was gassed. And, oh shit, is that lice in my daughter's hair?

Mother. Eff.

I quickly texted my ex-husband, who texted me back even more quickly that there was no way he could have her at his house with lice. Neither could my mom. And neither could anyone else. I had to take her with me or cancel my interview. Canceling was not an option. The job was too big, the league was too big, to just cancel because of lice. And I didn't have lice, so, I got on the phone and called every daycare within walking distance of the National Hockey League. Finally, I found one nearby that would take a child with head lice, if she had been treated and there were no visible adult lice. It was the same policy as Savannah's elementary school (which was put in place so that low-income districts could keep kids in school). Perfect.

I treated her, packed her up, and headed off to New York. She stared in awe as we crossed from New Jersey to the Big Apple through the Holland Tunnel. Her small face pressed against the glass as she tipped her head back . . . back . . . back . . . to see the tops of the buildings.

"It's like a million Columbuses." She exhaled a slow breath as her small hand touched the window. My heart caught in my chest. She saw the promise of a dream and a life bigger than her childlike heart had ever imagined. No matter what happened next, she saw a bigger world. She knew it was out there. She knew she could touch it and feel it and want it. And that's exactly what I wanted for her.

We easily breezed through the city, starting with the NHL headquarters so I could scout the area and parking spaces. Then we went to the Statue of Liberty and toured the city, taking in the steam rising from the grates and the hot dog vendors and the two-dollar T-shirts on every corner and the one-thousand-dollar couture they stood in front of. Savannah fell in love with the lights and the pigeons, which were her favorite thing about New York. She loved the notion of birds walking on the sidewalks with people, as though that's how it should always be.

We were dreamy-eyed and inspired by the time we returned to our cheap hotel in Jersey, which was just across the river. The breathtaking view of the city was the backdrop to the ten dollar pizza we picked up on the way back to the room. I was certain this move would be right for us. Being able to live in my favorite city felt like the payoff for all the pain and all the struggle I had gone through. This was where I could finally prove myself to anyone and everyone who had ever doubted that I could achieve big things.

When I got up the next morning, the peace of the day before was gone and was replaced with the familiar anxiety of days past. I was wound up so tight I thought I was going to spin off my feet. But I was determined to go to this interview no matter what. Savannah and I got ready and crossed through the Holland Tunnel, which had been a dream the night before but was now backed up for miles. The real New York was emerging. The traffic put me forty-five minutes off schedule, which meant I was going to be twenty minutes late to my interview. So, I texted Mr. NHL to let him know.

As I approached the daycare, I glanced over, and I saw it. That little bastard. That dumb, gross, little bastard scurrying across my daughter's hair.

Mother. Eff.

I couldn't take my adult-lice-infested daughter to the daycare, nor could I take her into NHL headquarters with me.

Wait, can I take her into NHL headquarters?
No, you cannot take her into NHL
headquarters with you!

Taking a deep breath, I looked over at her and smiled as the horns honked from the bustling NYC traffic.

The same energy we had loved only a day ago, now felt stifling as the panic set in. I had no one to call, nowhere to go, and no childcare options. More importantly, I realized this sort of thing would happen again if I moved to the city. If I needed help here, who would I call? My support network would be at least twelve hours away rather than two. My breath caught in my chest as my hands tightened around the steering wheel.

Shit.

"How about we go get ice cream in New Jersey, feed a few pigeons, and head home?" I blinked back the tears.

"Okay," she said. She didn't see my tears because she was looking out the window to find more pigeons.

As I looked down at my phone to make the call I didn't want to make, I accidentally crossed the wrong bridge into the wrong part of town, where the NYPD was doing a drug bust.

Well, New York, aren't you just a miserable wench.

The minute I turned my back, the Big Apple stuck a knife in it, taking back all the promises she

113

had made just hours ago. I pulled to a stop as an NYPD officer checked out my license plates, then came to my window.

"Need some help?" he asked. He'd probably assessed from my Ohio plates that I was in the wrong place.

I choked out the words and fought back tears. "I just . . . need the . . . Holland Tunnel."

"Oh, geez, lady." He told me where to go, but when I got there, the road was closed. New York was giving me the middle finger. After another hour and one more NYPD officer, I made it to New Jersey.

Finally, I made the call to Mr. NHL that I had been dreading. "I just can't." He listened as I explained my concerns about childcare. Who would I call for help? And the hours for this job were evening ones because the teams played at night. While I had initially ignored this fact amid my excitement, I was now immersed in the real NYC and wondering how to manage it. Not that I couldn't figure it out, I just didn't realize how hard it would be. Thankfully, he understood. As a parent in the big city, he knew what I was struggling with and didn't fault me for it. So, we parted on good terms with the hope for future possibilities.

Just a month later, Mr. NHL called again. "I've got something different. This is a day job. It's more money. And it may be a better fit."

I called Genevieve, my all-time confidante, and told her the news.

114

"What am I going to do? I want to go, but . . ." But I had a hard time believing it would work.

"You're going," Genevieve said. "You'll regret it if you don't. And this time, I'm driving."

And she did. From Columbus, Ohio, to New York City, she drove my stick shift so I could prep for my new interview. She dedicated the song "Everlasting Shine Blockaz," a mash-up of the Black Keys and Big Boi, to our road trip. We played it over and over on I-70 to the East Coast.

"I'm sure you'll get the job." She smiled at me from the driver's seat as her shiny locks lit up under the highway lights.

The next morning, the friend who had heard every one of my dreams drove me into the city and dropped me off at NHL headquarters to chase a new opportunity. I clutched my portfolio of work with a renewed sense of excitement in my veins.

You can do this, Stephanie. You can get the job. You can figure it out.

I waved goodbye with a huge smile. "Have fun!" I yelled.

"Don't worry. It's New York. I'll find something to do." She waved back as she headed off into the unknown.

I smiled as the wind whipped my hair. Straightening my shoulders, I headed into the large brick building, through security, and into the elevator.

115

When the doors opened, I stepped into the steel-covered offices of the NHL's New York City headquarters as its slick, black animated logo played on loop on the front entrance television. The steel was so massive it shocked me into silence. Standing in the middle of that kind of power and strength and legend took my breath away.

With hockey, I felt like part of an exclusive club. Or a brotherhood. A family. Maybe for the first time in my thirty-five years of life, I felt included in something bigger. This was a world into which many could only dream of being admitted. I understood the privilege of having a ticket, and was grateful for it.

It hadn't been easy to become a part of this family. I had known nothing about hockey when I started. I read *Hockey for Dummies*, watched the NHL's Greatest Hits videos, and scoured the writings of my peers so that I could learn the language, the players, the coaches, and the traditions. Like why Detroit throws octopuses on our ice and how the hell they smuggled it in Nationwide Arena, anyway.

Fittingly, I had fought my way into the ranks. I started at the furthest corner of the press box on the right side, where people who were virtually unknown would sit, and worked my way to the left side, where almost everyone in the press area knew me. I was honored to be a storyteller of this new world with its plot twists, heroes, guffaws, and villains.

116

The world of sports is colorful, complete with intrigue and passion and larger-than-life characters. People struggled to make it to the top as other people dealt with hitting rock bottom. Hockey players, who were just like every other person I'd ever interviewed for any other story, were out there doing their jobs. But they weren't like everyone else because their every move was endlessly scrutinized by all the news outlets, including the one I worked for. The public stripped them of their humanness, expecting them to be greater than human. Except there is no such thing. They were just people trying to do the best they could.

And here I am, trying to do the best I can.

I stepped into Mr. NHL's office and the interview began.

* * *

On our way back to Ohio that night, Genevieve laughed easily from the driver's seat. "I'm so proud of you, La Steph."

Her enthusiasm was about me but also about her. We both had a desire to escape the Midwest for a bit. To step outside the world of motherhood and jobs and life, even if just for a moment. I didn't have the heart to tell the person who had been through so much with me what I already knew in my gut—I didn't get the job. I just smiled and nodded as we

117

drove the ten hours home, hoping against hope that maybe, just maybe, I was wrong.

Genevieve was the first person I called two weeks later when the news officially rolled in. She was the only one who would truly understand the spirited energy of New York and the subsequent monotony when returning to adulthood, kids, single parenting, and jobs.

I will never get an opportunity like this again.

"It wasn't meant to be," Genevieve said.

I knew when I walked into NHL headquarters that two things were going to happen: (1) I was going to interview my ass off, and (2) I wouldn't hide my single mother status. I had never hidden it because it was wholly who I was, and I was proud of my commitment to the notion. So, my answer was clear when the interviewer asked me something along the lines of, "How do you plan on navigating New York with no support system as a single mother?"

"Nothing and no one comes before my daughter," I said. I was stoic as I explained that I, as a single mother, would sometimes have to leave in the middle of work to go get her, leave early to pick her up, or come in late because I had to take her somewhere. Standard parenting procedure. I would work hard, which Mr. NHL knew; but I came with strings, which he found out.

Since the day she was born, I had never wavered from my stance that she came first. Sacrificing even a second of her life for anything or anyone was never part of the plan, and I was upfront about that. I was not the woman many in the sports world wanted me to be: a starry-eyed, blonde-haired ditz. (Sadly, that was also a reputation that came with my weight loss). I was a mother who was serious about securing a better life and bigger dreams for my daughter than I'd had growing up.

It's an unpopular stance to have, of course. People wanted me to act the way I looked with my new body: like I should only be thinking about marriage, money, and sex. I did think about those things (of course), but they were not my primary objectives. My singular thought on a perpetual loop was Savannah and how I was going to feed her, clothe her, and get her a better life. It gave all my employers, family, and friends fits. It gave me fits.

The truth was, the NHL would always be there, but my daughter would not always be nine years old. Or ten. Or eleven. Or twelve. If she was sick, it wasn't that I had to pick her up, I wanted to pick her up. If she had to go to the ER, I wanted to take her. I wanted to be the mom that reads to her kid at night, drops her off and picks her up from school, and is present in her life. I wanted her to know that nothing was more important than she was. Ever. Not my looks, not my marital status, and not my bank account.

On the other hand, companies don't have to care about the state of my motherhood or if I'm a good parent or not. Could Mr. NHL find talent equal to mine but with less strings attached?

Yep.

And I could not fault him for that. I was, to most employers, a liability because I was a single mother. Had I already been embedded in New York, the story might have ended differently. I had the resume and the work ethic. I was committed to any job I had, but only so far as it didn't interfere with raising my daughter.

Being committed to my vision of motherhood didn't make it any easier to lose out on jobs or boyfriends or life experiences. I've never understood how I could feel so right in my decisions and so devastated all at the same time. Both emotions occupied the same amount of space in my mind and battled for the right to be there. Except both had the right to be there.

I was feeling the push and pull. The world demanded that I be there for my kid but punished me when I was. Mr. NHL wanted to hire me for my abilities, but as a hiring manager, he was battling something bigger than himself. Bigger than the NHL. Even as far as women had come, our society still hadn't been able to answer the work/life balance question that is unique to mothers and women. And since most hiring managers can't change the larger issues at play, they must deal with it at the individual level. In other words, Mr. NHL knew how that specific job worked, and once he knew how I worked, he realized the two were incompatible. And that was it.

However, had he offered me the job, I might have made the same choice for myself and my daughter, as evidenced by that first unsuccessful trip to New York. No matter how hard individuals and organizations tried to equalize the world for women and mothers, they were slamming up against a society that was just not built for women and mothers. Our society was built by, and for, men. Trying to give women access to that infrastructure is like trying to give ships access to highways. Highways weren't built for ships, just like the world wasn't built for women. The world needed to be rebuilt, and whose job was that?

I imagined for a moment my mother in the same position when I was Savannah's age. She was battling the push and pull too. In order to be a better provider for me and my brother, she had to go back to nursing school. But that meant she had to leave me alone, night and day, at the tender age of ten. It was not her wish or her dream, but it was her reality. On her own, even with a nursing degree, she couldn't put me in the right place with the right connections and opportunities to make a difference in my life. She could only feed me, clothe me, and give me a place to rest my head. Everything else was up to me.

121

That upbringing only heightened my sense of urgency to do right by Savannah, who did have an advantage: she had me. And she had yet to discover that I would go to extraordinary lengths to fight for her right to a better life.

"It'll all work out," Genevieve said with a knowing spirit. "You're La Steph! On to the next adventure."

And she was right.

A short time later, as I anxiously watched my print journalist friends get laid off one-by-one, a new opportunity presented itself. I was offered a social media position at a company in Columbus. I'd work during the day within a manageable distance to my daughter's school. It seemed, on the surface, like a perfect job.

The same week, Fox Sports Ohio hired me to write for their website and appear on-air for its show *Blue Jackets Live*.

With that, the new adventure had begun.

But that adventure was not as intriguing as the man about to enter my life.

Chapter 13
Lightning Strike

Author Candace Bushnell gave Carrie Bradshaw her Mr. Big in *Sex and the City*, and now I had mine.

The first time my Mr. Big—let's call him Sandalwood—touched me, I started to change from the inside out. I was chatting with a coworker when he breezed by and lightly touched my outer arm saying, "Hey you," before smiling and walking out the door. I felt a sharp bolt of energy from his touch that hit my insides with a shocking contraction. The transfer of electricity elicited a small gasp from me.

"Uh," was all I could get out. I watched him walk out before glancing at the guy next to me, who just raised an eyebrow and smiled. Had he felt that current, too? He must have. Like when you walk in a room and you can quickly root out who's sleeping together simply by their intimate glances, their angled bodies, and their passing touches. Their electricity glows brighter the closer that they get to each other. And then lightning strikes.

Was it possible a piece of who I was could exist in another person? Not that he completed me, but that he had an answer to a question I didn't know to ask yet. That something in him was integral to finding something in me. Anytime I was near him, I glowed. Energy. And the transference of it.

He smelled like a fresh shower and, sometimes, a light scent of sandalwood. He was sturdy and masculine, and I liked that. For years now, I'd been required to be only a mother. Around him, I could just be a woman with needs of her own. He felt like someone who could meet those needs easily with adept hands and a slow burn that was intoxicating. But unlike the simple sexual chemistry I had with Mr. Athlete, Mr. Sandalwood and I had the animal attraction and so much more. After two years of seeing him around and getting to know him beyond that physical attraction, I came to love very specific things about him and who he was. The thing I loved best was that he softened my edges. Oh, and his laugh. That gorgeous laugh.

He laughed with an effervescent baritone that tickled my ears and was undeniably his and his alone. I watched his bright eyes sparkle and felt like I could tap into that well of happiness and safely extract the lightness behind it. His eyes always seemed to be laughing, even when he wasn't, which had been a foreign concept to me since I was a child. I'd always had a hard time laughing and even speaking.

"Such a serious little girl," my mother always said with a bit of disappointment on her face. She wanted me to be lighter, somehow. She wanted my soul to lose its darkness. To chit-chat on the phone with her endlessly about meaningless things like whether it would be a cold winter, and did I hear

124

about Uncle so-and-so? I did it because it was my mother and I loved her, but underneath it all I didn't want to talk at all unless there was a purpose. Everything had to have its reason, or why do it at all?

Sandalwood was my relief from that. A relief from how serious I was. He was my way out of a darkened soul. I would watch him—no, study him—from quiet corners of our shared workspace and marvel at how laughter bubbled out of him like champagne on New Year's Eve. Mirth tumbling out of him as though it was the most natural thing in the world to gush with happiness over the tiniest things.

I had never laughed like that, but I wanted to. I lived in the darkest part of the ocean, where still waters ran deep and cold, numbing me in ways that felt dangerous to myself and others. It felt like being submerged without air and struggling to break the surface. I tried to resist the blackness inside me but could not deny its existence.

The lightness inside him gave life to me, and I could feel myself coming up for air. If I believed in reincarnation, I would tell you that I had known him for many lives, and we always arrived at this moment together, somewhere in time, and forever. His presence was a comfortable, strong I've-been-here-before-with-you feeling. He was familiar to me in ways even I didn't understand. I breathed in relief and exhaled anxiety every time I was near him, as though he had known my soul from its first bright moment and taken care of it ever since.

125

I could do no wrong in his eyes. He was a constant ear to speak in, a sturdy body to lean on, and an open heart that understood me in a way no one ever had. For the first time in my life, I was in the presence of someone who got how big my dreams were. Not only did he get it, but he knew intimately the pathway to reach them. He had big dreams, too, and had worked hard to reach them. Feeling known was a powerful experience. That made him larger than life to me. And I was enamored with him.

But my friends and family were worried he was a snake charmer or a good salesman, and they tried their best to dissuade me from involving myself with him. "He's going to hurt you," said Mr. Politico.

"Probably," I said.

But I loved his sales pitch. Plus, he wasn't selling to me, right? I was different. It had been love at first sight. What could go wrong?

So, I sat with him in a darkened theater for a movie of my choosing, knowing this was the beginning of something.

"This is for us," he said as he offered me popcorn.

I breathed him in as his eyes sparkled even in the darkened theater. I craved his touch so much it felt like I was vibrating. Sensing this, his hand found my thigh again. This time I leaned into his shoulder and found the crook of his neck.

There was something both carnivorous and comforting about the crook of his neck. Where the curve met the collarbone is the one place I found both solace and lust. In a moment, I went from sweet innocence to scandalous passion. And sure enough, it was only a moment before his lips were on mine, and the world was dead to me as my body came alive.

My head and my heart were changed in that moment. Before, I had been drifting. Now, I was colliding with something that was either going to sink me or save me. For the first time, in a long time, I could feel something. The numbness that had permeated my life was gone. In its place was something very warm and very real that thawed the ice lodged in my veins. He could make the whole world melt away. There was just him and a peaceful quiet as his breath warmed my neck.

I remember watching a game on TV with him, cuddling on my couch. Feeling his arm around me was the most intoxicating sensation. He wrapped me in tight and lightly ran his fingers up and down my arm. I slid my hand just under his T-shirt and let it rest on his stomach. We talked and laughed and kissed. We were passionately entwined in each other.

I could imagine a million days and nights with him just like that. So much so, that I allowed myself to imagine what it might be like to have him around even more, maybe even around Savannah. What would that look like? It was the first time since my divorce that I had imagined incorporating someone into mine and Savannah's life in that way.

Savannah and I were the *Gilmore Girls*, and that's the way I wanted it. Sandalwood had become the Luke Danes to my Lorelei Gilmore. The relationship suited me nicely because Savannah had a father, and I had no reason to replace him. He loved her, and while we had a complicated relationship (as exes tend to have), I had zero interest in bringing in some guy and saying, "Here's your new daddy, Savannah!" The character of Luke Danes understood that.

Just like Lorelei, I had taken great pride over the years in proving that I could do it all by myself. Savannah and I would be just fine, thank you. That started to change when I asked Sandalwood to help me move a coffee table that I, for months, could not get centered in my living room. In a matter of seconds, we set it right. Suddenly, I thought differently about my situation. The more time I spent with him, domesticated and intimate, the more vulnerable I became. But I was painfully aware that I had fallen much faster than he had.

I didn't want to say out loud what was really on my mind: "I'm scared I'm the only one who's falling," or "I'm scared he only thinks of me for sex," or "I don't want to be rejected," or "I don't think he likes me," or "He doesn't even know my middle name and I love him. I am stupid." The battle between intellect and heart, between the what-I-know-to-be-true and what-I-wish-to-be-true, was in full swing.

128

In reality, he was going through a divorce. I was with the separated man. I knew that if I pushed too hard, I would be the rebound girl. And if I didn't push hard enough, I would be nothing. So, I did very little. I waited for him to work through his dissolving marriage and removed myself from the situation unless he called. But in doing so, I placed myself in an orbit that revolved around his life only. It didn't align with what I really wanted and needed, and then the text.

That damn text.

"Siren," he texted me in the middle of a random conversation. In his mind, it was a compliment to my sexuality and the way that I looked. In my mind, it was an insult. The sudden realization of what we were started to sink into my bones. He was calling me what I was to him: a sexual conquest. But to me, this relationship had meant so much more: I was hurting because I loved him.

The recognition of the gap between us was heartbreaking. I was in the throes of unrequited love, which is the worst kind of love. The kind that breaks your heart and lasts forever, leaving you in a constant spiral of "Why didn't this person love me?" and "What could I have done differently?"

Sandalwood had changed my insides. But to him, I was a distraction. A lovely possession to get him through his divorce, not a human to love. He wanted flirtation and lightness. I wanted meaningful conversations. Somehow, though, we could never get

129

past, "Hey beautiful," the phrase that explicitly expressed what he thought of me.

Maybe being this thin was not the blessing I had hoped for. When I was married, I was heavy, but I was loved. I hadn't been able to say that since then, and I was the thinnest I had ever been. Was it possible that I had become a new type of woman? Could the way I looked be enticing a new type of man for the new type of woman that I appeared to be? Was it possible that thinness only guaranteed quantity and not quality? Yes, I was attracting more men. Yes, I had attracted Sandalwood. But what was my return on investment?

My return to reality was jarring. Emails and doctor's appointments and school plays and sunsets and sunrises were constant interruptions to the looping video in my mind. A video that constantly recapped those precious moments with him when I was allowed to just be a woman, not a mother or a breadwinner or a trophy. His larger-than-life presence exuded a light and energy that comforted and confounded me.

I wanted to believe there was more between us. In fact, the desire to believe something that was only a little bit true was perhaps more addictive than he was. Hope was potent, and it was decadent to wrap myself in the comfort of an illusion. The silky feel of it was better than the cold possibility he might never feel the same way I did.

But until I knew for sure, there was nothing more for me here. Our relationship was over and he was gone. For now.

Chapter 14
Illusion Deconstructed

Nearly four months after Sandalwood and I stopped talking, I heard from him again. By this time, his divorce was a few months from being final. The night he called, he invited me to his home.

"Just please meet me out," he said.

The minute I pulled into his driveway, he jumped at me like a big, golden retriever. The joy and laughter that had marked the beginning of our relationship returned. It reminded me of the electricity I felt four years ago when I met him. It reminded me of the happiness that had filled me two years ago when he kissed me for the first time. And I remembered why I had entered this relationship in the first place—that connection. He had something beautiful inside him, something inherently good, and something I loved. Yes, it was love. Some kind of love. Then I remembered why it stopped: he didn't love me back. Sometimes, it didn't even feel like he liked me back, at least not in any way beyond being the siren he claimed I was.

Unrequited. I felt stupid. And I didn't want to feel stupid anymore for thinking this was more than it was, for not knowing what it was, and for not being able to talk about it. But now I sat in a bar with him, confused and uncertain.

"Why me?" I asked as all my other words failed me. He had targeted me like I was a clay

132

pigeon at some shooting event where he pulled the trigger and broke me into smithereens. He'd put a bullseye on my back. But why?

"I don't really know," he said. "There was just something about you, every time I was near you."

He said that from the first time he met me, he had felt something. And he thought I was beautiful.

"You just gave me that feeling." He looked in my eyes with a smoldering intensity.

Immediately, I remembered the I-want-you stances and the sultry stares he had tossed my way. The energy and electricity that seemed to zap between us whenever we were close to each other was indisputable.

"I just felt a connection."

I wasn't sure I wanted him to see what was behind my eyes, knowing it was far more than what was behind his, so I looked away. When I couldn't get my words out, he kept going.

He said he kept feeling that connection, time and again, and that intrigued him. Then he found out I was more than a pretty face. I had some substance, and that intrigued him most of all.

"And I've been on a quest ever since then to figure out what this is." He gestured between us.

I had waited all this time to hear exactly that from him. For so long, I'd wanted him to realize that our relationship was about more than just a sexual

133

attraction and that I was more than a siren. It felt wonderful to be able to tell him that I felt that spark, too.

Then we talked. Really talked. For the first time, he let me into his inner world. He told me all about his family, his parents, his exes, and his kids. I told him about my family, my marriage, and my divorce. And we connected.

"What kind of music do you like?" he asked during a pause in this deep conversation.

"All kinds."

"Me, too." He smiled as he showed me his playlists, which included children's songs for his kids—much like the ones I had for Savannah—and one of my favorite songs, "At Last," by Etta James.

"I love that song!" I pointed at his iTunes list.

"Me, too." He laughed as he scrolled through his songs.

"You know if you download Spotify, you can create tons of lists without having to buy every song."

"I'll have to try it," he said as silence blanketed our little spot in the world.

I glanced at him, and then I felt it.

Something wasn't right. I couldn't put my finger on it. I was thrilled to be there with him. I knew I loved him. In some way. But maybe it was the lateness of the call, or the fact he'd been out all day drinking at a local event with his buddies, or the fact he'd kept me on the hook for so long, or the fact I'd let him do it, or the fact that even after all this time I still couldn't tell him the way I really felt. It might have been that I knew he'd been with other women during the time we were apart. That other people knew what he was doing, but I knew nothing about his comings and goings. I don't know. But the authenticity of the moment felt betrayed, somehow. I sat at that bar, stifled. Not by him, but by my own hand.

After we left the bar, I dropped him off at home, and for the first time since this relationship started, he asked me to spend the night with him. He was being open. Asking me in. I said no.

I just didn't know which guy he was—was he a Mr. High School or a Mr. Husband? Not knowing the answer meant I didn't trust him with my body. I didn't trust that once he got what he wanted, whatever that was, that he would keep me around. I didn't trust what he said. I didn't trust what he did. I didn't trust him. It was why we'd never had sex and why we weren't going to have it on this night either.

I had come into and walked out of many types of relationships in my life. Mr. Husband had been the first man I slept with, and we waited to have sex until we were in love and started to talk about marriage. After our divorce, I dated a lot. I did the flings, the one-night-stands, and even the one-night-stand morphing into a relationship that led to love. I

135

dated older guys and younger guys, athletes, accountants, techies, and artists.

And then there was Sandalwood. He was someone I could marry. He was someone I could see as a stepfather to my daughter and someone I could envision having a child with.

There were moments between us when it seemed like he felt the same way. When he looked at me a certain way or kissed me in a certain way. When he trusted me with himself and let me in. But as quickly as those feelings came, they were gone. And I could never trust that the man I might go to bed with would be the same man I woke up with.

He was, in part, enamored with the way I looked, but I already knew how that story ended. When we dated, I was at one of my thinnest weights and proud of myself for being strong and healthy. But I knew my historical struggle with weight. I knew that if I gained weight, he would pressure me to lose it so that I fit the role his lifestyle required. And I would wish to be free from all of that. It would be a constant fight about the way I looked, with the love of my life, for the rest of my life.

But then there were the parts of him I loved. The part that was equally enamored with who I was as a person, the way my brain worked, and how it made him feel to be with me. The part that loved having long, amorous phone conversations with me. The part that came to life when he saw me across a room. That's the man I was attracted to and wanted. The man who would do anything I asked of him.

But I never did ask for anything.

Because which man would dominate our relationship? Which man would show up when I was sick or hurt or overweight? I didn't know because Sandalwood and I, we had missed a step somewhere. We were not real. We were a figment of my imagination in the place where hope lived and where small gestures meant more than they should.

So, we said our goodbyes and my heart felt like a giant rock in the middle of my chest. I hauled it around inside me all day long while I put on the best show of my life to the public with my smile and my bright eyes. By now, I was an expert at wearing a mask.

But when the night came and I was alone and Savannah was in bed, my eyes would fill with tears. I would rehash repeatedly the two years of Sandalwood's now-you're-in-my-life, now-you're-not game.

This was the relationship, out of all the relationships I'd had on my journey, that stuck so profoundly in my mind. This brand of poison, which I had so easily chosen for myself, was the most potent of anything I had consumed yet. But no matter what happened next and no matter how much it hurt, he had changed me. I couldn't steal that from him. I couldn't take away the thing that we both knew was so special. He had really meant something to me.

137

Maybe more than anyone had before and in ways that no one had before.

More importantly, I couldn't steal that from myself. He had awakened me, opening something light and beautiful inside me. And even though the lovely moment we had together was gone, I would carry that light with me forever, knowing that I had given him everything I could give at the time. My sanity, my soul, and my heart.

Sandalwood made me re-think my life. No, he made me re-feel my life. He showed me how big life could be, and for that I was grateful. That's why he lingered in my soul, despite my protests, like a silent black and white film that plays on a loop in the background forever. He was the man who made me feel human again, which meant he was the one who could hurt me the most. So, I had to move on, even if it crushed me.

But this time, instead of turning to him or anyone else for answers, I looked inside myself. The lonely road ahead was going to be hard, but I was committed to the journey no matter how treacherous it became. I had Savannah to think about, after all. And she was my north star on our two-person voyage.

Chapter 15
Undercurrent

I was at a fork in the road. I hadn't anticipated I would have to choose between my life as I had envisioned it for myself and Savannah's life as I had envisioned it for her. I never thought the two would be mutually exclusive, but that's what they were quickly becoming. Living two lives—one as a single woman and one as a mom—had happened first with dating. And now, it was happening again with her education.

Savannah and I seemed, by all appearances, to be doing okay in our tiny loft apartment in German Village, which was just south of downtown Columbus. It reminded me of a mini-New York loft and neighborhood. We walked across the street for Greek food, down a block to play at the park, and up a few extra blocks for Jeni's ice cream when I had enough money.

In our tiny digs, Savannah and I shared the loft's bedroom with a skylight and one crimson wall where we hung her drawings. I'd write under the bright ceiling, with that red wall warming the light, while she played quietly with her stuffed animals, which occupied any space she had on her side of the room. I took comfort in hearing her breathe at night under the glittering snowflakes we'd made the year before and hung above her bed. We had made it this far, and this was our home.

Where we lived was, without a doubt, the most authentic representation of who I was. And I always wanted Savannah to have what I had, which was a blend of downtown smarts with country values. She was certainly getting that by living the city life with me and the country life with her dad and grandparents.

Despite my reasons for leaving all those years ago, I genuinely cherished my rural roots. I was grateful to the town and the people in it for instilling good values, a strong work ethic, and an appreciation for nature and its beauty. I loved the creek at the bottom of our hill and the land we would run on barefoot, feeling the cool grass on our worn toes. When I was in the city, as much as I loved it, I missed the country air and the down-home people who'd give you a cup of sugar if you needed it.

You did not take sugar from city neighbors or leave your doors (or house or car) unlocked at any time. Savannah was learning both of those lessons and finding comfort and things to love in both worlds, the same as me.

But as comfy as we had become in this quaint world of ours, I felt that fork in the road like a spear to my nerves. Not only was I dealing with saying goodbye to Sandalwood but I was at a point where I had to say goodbye to a huge part of my identity and what I wanted for myself. This was about Savannah, and I knew, from an education perspective, she needed more.

140

The elementary school we were in had been good to my daughter, there was no question. I was grateful for the teachers and cultural diversity we experienced. One teacher in particular, Ms. Wonderful, would watch Savannah after school. I was indebted to her for my financial stability because her generosity allowed me to work while she helped with childcare. She changed our lives for the better. And the neighborhood was so lovely too. We had many fond memories of our life there.

But in the fourth grade, Savannah had an experience with another child that shifted my viewpoint about where we were living. She had briefly stepped out of the lunch line, and when she tried to get back in, a boy who was stronger than her—who had been held back for two years— grabbed her by the shoulders and threw her against the wall, causing her head to slam back and hit the cement.

After she told me what happened, she admitted that she was also being bullied by other classmates. For Savannah, the kids who made fun of her for being smart outweighed the friends she had made and the life we were living downtown.

So, once she entered the fifth grade and was prepping for middle school, I started researching all the school districts in central Ohio. The most important criterion was for the school to have a proven reputation for sending graduates to good colleges. If college was Savannah's path, it was my

141

job to surround her with the right structure. Upper Arlington offered all these things, including a solid college recruitment reputation. Plus, its proximity to downtown made it a fair compromise for both our lives.

The issue then became, "How am I going to afford this district?" Residency was going to determine Savannah's future. That fact had informed my leaving Mr. Husband in the first place and the issue resurfaced now. I looked around me and recognized the privilege I had in being able to choose to move. So many of the parents around me didn't have that choice. It is the constant struggle of urban life in America. The families in these districts deserve a shot at the same quality of education they could find in the suburbs, but they don't always have the same access or tax dollars to create that equality. And the majority of them can't just pick up and move, nor would they want to.

I couldn't change the current system or its inequalities, but I could change my address. So, I did. Although I could afford to make the move to a new school district, I had concerns that eventually the financial expenses of such a wealthy neighborhood might do me in. I ignored my gut in favor of doing whatever I could to give Savannah the future I promised her.

I began perusing the Upper Arlington neighborhoods, trying to find my own little place in this new world. I started in the upscale

142

neighborhoods on the south end, which turned out to be far too rich for my blood. So, I drove to the north side of Upper Arlington, which was filled with more middle-class families. This is where my soul felt at home. There was grit in the dirty pickup trucks, Toyotas, and the Hondas. These were middle-class people who wanted a better life for their kids, same as I wanted for mine. Signing the lease let us in. And that was that.

I felt I was doing the right thing for Savannah. By moving to this area, I was giving her an education that could change the course of her life. It was a move that was completely in line with what I had set out to do when I left. Education is one elixir to a diseased system that tries its hardest to keep women in their place. I was the first person in my nuclear family to get a bachelor's degree, and it had opened doors for me. My mother wasn't as lucky. Her high school diploma and one semester of college barely kept my brother and I going in government-subsidized housing after she left my father. And even the technical, LPN-education she worked so hard for during those lean years was never enough to pull us out of poverty. She did her best, but ultimately, getting remarried was what changed our zip code. Without that union, we would have simply disappeared into the background.

It was, in fact, my stepfather who impressed upon me the importance of college and insisted on paying for that education. Without him, it's hard to tell where I would have ended up. No one in my immediate sphere had a college degree: not my mom, not my dad, not my brother, and not my grandparents. We were a classic American, military, blue-collar family on both sides and proud of it. But I wanted something different.

My stepfather's influence that changed the course of my life. So, in turn, I would change the course of my daughter's life through a good education, even if it cost me everything. And I knew that it would.

By now, there was a shaky undercurrent running through our lives. I could feel its low vibration starting to shake my world apart. After the move I started to miss my downtown life. Or more accurately, I missed the way that life made me feel. Where we had been living in German Village had become my whole identity and now it was gone. The new suburban life felt too rich for my blood, even though it was exactly what Savannah needed. She made friends instantly, and they became a tight-knit group. She excelled in her classes, and her personality started to flourish.

I had put Savannah at the center of my decision, and it was the absolute right choice. For her.

But that low-level current of uncertainty never went away. I was struggling with the identity change and that gnawing feeling of being right on the verge of financial collapse. It had never left me. It caused me to overcorrect financially and work extreme hours to try and maintain the life I had chosen for my daughter. I was, at one point, working five jobs for almost ninety hours a week, plus raising Savannah, missing Sandalwood, losing a large chunk of my identity, all without steady support or even a break. I started to crack under the pressure, recognizing that I had extended myself, my emotions, and my finances well beyond their limits.

At the same time, I didn't feel secure in my job. I now realized that the company I worked for, which I had left sports and journalism for, was a shaky foundation to build a life on. I thought things would get better, but in fact, they got worse. Much worse. And I was absolutely struggling to keep my head above water. The pressure to keep this job and maintain this façade was increasing at a pace that I couldn't keep up with. The anxiety and depression from days past started to thread through my muscles.

How am I going to keep this life going if I lose my job?

The issue centered around my supervisor, who was making coy advances towards me (and flirting with my coworkers), which I dealt with as just part of the game that women play in the professional world. After all, I had always worked in male-dominated environments and understood how things operated. In order to be considered equal to a man, a woman must be cunning and intelligent, playing six steps ahead and working ten times harder than the men while simultaneously smiling and flirting as though it's part of the job description. Most of the jobs I had worked, including this one, always had a subtle intimation that, in the presence of men, I should appear less smart, less ambitious, and less likely to report unprofessional behavior to HR. I felt like my job depended on dumbing myself down. And the pressure to be the cool girl, who laughed it all off unlike all those other angry feminist girls, was palpable.

I had learned in my professional life that when a woman complains, she's told it's her fault, and she suffers the consequences while the man gets promoted. This is a direct result of our society's attitude of victim shaming and blaming, which is propagated by the same men who do the damage in the first place. And for me, a strong, opinionated women, I also felt the wrath of being too assertive, too opinionated, and too ambitious. These, of course, are traits of good leaders, but only if you're a man. If you're a woman, these traits are examples of being pushy, inflexible, and coming on too strong.

I was a single mother with a daughter to raise, and I had too much to lose. So, what was I going to do about my supervisor's latest inappropriate behavior, knowing that it wasn't the first or last time I'd have to deal with it? Fight the whole damn system? I had done that through journalism, and it had taken its toll personally and professionally. The reality was that I had to put food

146

on the table, buy clothes, pay for my car, and keep my place in Savannah's school district, and I could barely do that.

So, I tolerated my supervisor's behavior. *This is just how it is.*

Adding to the complexity of what was happening at work was the fact that my boss had gone to bat for me. Apparently, in my journalist days, I had written an article that someone at the company didn't like. We'll call this someone Mr. Glib. When Mr. Glib found out my boss had hired me, he asked my boss to fire me before I even started. My boss refused and then told me about it on my first day of work as if I owed him something. This created a strange dynamic between us because I immediately felt beholden to him.

Being a former journalist, I sought out confirmation from trusted friends within the company. They verified what my boss told me: Mr. Glib did not like me and said I would never work in his department.

I was not entirely surprised by Mr. Glib's hostility. It's always a possible side effect of being a journalist. When you spend your life dissecting people for all the world to see, you don't typically make a lot of friends. And once you leave that job, the power dynamic shifts. The people you wrote about suddenly have power over you, and how they choose to use it is up to them. Mr. Glib was exercising his right to be vengeful.

147

So, now I was dealing with a double-whammy situation. On one front, there was Mr. Glib's retribution and his enormous influence over others in the company. On the other front, there was my boss, whom I was now indebted to for my job, and his flirtatious behavior within a team of young, attractive females he'd personally hired. At one point (as I was told) he called us his Charlie's Angels.

Together, he and Mr. Glib created an environment of isolation for me. Who could I trust? I couldn't turn to anyone outside of our department because Mr. Glib's stories about me had poisoned the water. But I also couldn't turn to my boss, who had given me the job and was flirting with me.

So, I negotiated my future at every turn, working harder, faster, and smarter than most to make up for Mr. Glib's negativity and to counteract any flirtations from my boss. For two years, I did everything I was supposed to do right up until the moment when the raise and promotion I had earned—and was promised—was given to two younger, attractive females with a, "Sorry, keep up the good work," from my boss.

The stress of working in this environment, my inability to transfer to a different department within the company (which I was more than qualified for) because of Mr. Glib, and having my promised income stripped away, was wearing on me. Although this was not the first time my financial security was jeopardized because of men in power, it was the most egregious. If I played along, I would be jeopardizing my sense of worth and my income. If I did not play along, I would be jeopardizing my ability to get a job in Columbus (given each man's contacts, influence, and power). I was a single mother with a child to think about, and men with power controlled my every move. It was stifling.

I now had chronic fatigue, I wasn't sleeping, and my panic attacks had increased. My chest was always tight, and my muscles hurt. I started to get angry, just as a way of being, not over anything specific. But when there was something specific, I'd over-react to it with hellfire fury.

People started to look at me funny, wondering where it was coming from. I couldn't explain because even I couldn't fully understand it. I only knew that I had always been the go-to girl. People could rely on me, especially in a crisis, to turn something over fast, whether it was an article or a press release or a project. I was speedy. I worked hard. I had a solid work ethic. And that was undeniable.

But now I was the one in crisis. I was the one who needed a go-to person. But no one knew what to do with me because I wasn't the me they knew. My smiles were lost to tears, enthusiasm lost to depression, care and concern lost to anxiety and resentment. Anger was the ruling king of the tyrannical society within my mind.

I was imploding. I couldn't sustain the facade. The illusion was colliding with the reality. I couldn't be Super Mom or Super Worker or Super Friend or Super Daughter or Super Woman or Super Siren anymore. I felt beaten, defeated, and destroyed. My life was still not my own.

My female friendships started to break down as well. The dynamic of married versus single, of two incomes versus one, and of parent versus non-parent was cracking the foundations I thought were so secure. Girlfriends thought I wanted their husbands. (I didn't.) Girlfriends, whose husbands allowed them to be financially secure, were annoyed that I couldn't afford to be part of the same things they could. (I was broke.) And a girlfriend yelled at me for not attending a birthday party at a bar. (I was home with Savannah and couldn't afford a babysitter or even a beer.) Our differences started to chip away at me.

I loved my girlfriends. I loved all of them for who they were and what they stood for. I would do anything for my friends, but the reverse proved not to be true, save a handful of women. The differences between us were hard to overcome. And as one friend put it, she didn't want to deal with my so-called "drama."

It's easy to have a million girlfriends when you're in your twenties and thirties because you want to experience different people and allow them to inform who you are. But as you move into your late thirties, forties, and fifties, you start to know yourself

150

better. Having children accelerates this process. As each of you becomes busy with your own lives, children, partners, or careers, the process of knowing what you like and don't like becomes clearer. You start to weed out those relationships that may not fit anymore. And girlfriends in crisis can become a liability to perfectly styled lives, making them easy to remove regardless of what they're going through.

That was me, Ms. Removed.

I started eating a lot. And I started gaining weight. Normally, in these kinds of situations, I would go for a run, where I could drown all my problems in adrenaline and walk away feeling better. That was how I lost all the weight in the first place, and how I maintained that weight loss. But now the depression was so overwhelming that I couldn't get myself to go to the gym. So, I did nothing but eat and apply for jobs to get me out of the stressful situation I was in at work.

The tranquility of the world Savannah and I had built downtown was gone, and in its place was a terrifying undercurrent that was about to pull me under. I could see the end coming but had no ability to stop it.

I was about to drown.

And I was going to pull my daughter down with me.

Chapter 16
Middle School Homeless

Looking in the mirror had become the hardest part of my day. This was my reflection but not my bathroom or my home. I was permitted to use the address to get my mail, but beyond that, nothing here was mine except the two mattresses, three cats, four suitcases, and one middle school-aged daughter.

We had gone under, but we knew how to swim. No matter what happened next, I had done the right thing.

I reported my boss to Human Resources, explaining the multiple incidents I'd had with him and speaking up about what I'd seen him do to other women as well. Turns out, I was not the only one who objected to his behavior. I was just one of a long list of females who had similar experiences and decided to take action.

The decision to report him was not clear-cut. I wish it had been. It would have been easier and cleaner to say, "This is a bad guy. Punish him." But even as I was talking to HR, I found myself walking into the gray areas and giving context to what I was saying. I did not believe he was a bad person. I believe he made bad decisions for bad reasons because he was human, like all of us. And I believed that he had the ability to change.

So, before I said anything to anyone, I tried to think of all the times I had made bad decisions, the reasons I made them, and the people I hurt. When I went into the HR meeting, I put that same context around what I was reporting. I wasn't trying to hurt him; I was trying to stop him from continuing to hurt me. And from hurting the younger women in our organization. But the biggest reason I reported it was because of my daughter. When I looked at my young female coworkers, I saw my daughter in them.

If one of them was my daughter, what would I want a woman in my position to do about this?

The answer to that question pushed me into reporting him. It was the first time in my professional life I had reported a man for poor behavior, and I felt myself crossing over from the cool girl who puts up with it to the feminist woman who no longer would. Crossing that bridge was terrifying because when women speak up, when women report things, when women say no and ask for help, they are the ones who are put on trial. Child or no child, reporting him felt like a huge risk to take personally and professionally.

But when I saw those young women in the office and when I saw my daughter at home knowing she was on her way into the professional world, it felt like not saying anything at all was the bigger risk to take and would have a much larger impact. I felt like I had tape over my mouth when I was molested and when I was assaulted. I didn't want to feel like that anymore. I tore off the tape and accepted what was to come.

153

Shortly thereafter, my boss met with HR to learn his fate, and I took a job in a different department. It was not where I wanted to be because I was still blacklisted from my preferred team by Mr. Glib, so I decided to leave the company.

A short-lived bright spot during this time (other than HR doing its job well) was being hired by a small, upstart agency and believing it was a new beginning. Unfortunately, a few weeks into it, I found out I was dealing with an older, white male who was controlled by a young, attractive female on his team. This time around, I was upfront, honest, direct, and kind but firm about what I was experiencing (again). She didn't like that, so he fired me.

It would become a theme in my life as I got older and my female coworkers got younger. The dynamic of an older man in a position of power hiring young women and ousting older ones never failed to disappointment. And it was, once again, an example of women being pitted against each other instead of men being held accountable for the pitting.

The major difference between the two companies was the Human Resources Department. At my previous company, the HR staff—first and foremost—believed me when I told them what happened, and then they acted immediately to stop it. That attitude was invaluable to my ability as a woman to keep my job and not have to play to men to do it. The smaller agency, with no real HR presence, made the same issue impossible to fight.

The experience made me think about women in smaller companies without a Human Resources Department or without a well-run human resources department. What happened to them when they were dealt the same hand? Society tells women to stand up and defend themselves in the face of discrimination or mistreatment. But if she has no one who believes her, if she has no one who has her back, and nothing except her word to stand on, then what?

That question stared me in the face as I was forced into unemployment. Over the next year, I applied for over one hundred jobs and gained one hundred pounds. Out of the one hundred job applications, I got four interviews and zero offers.

Every day became the worst day of my life. My psychologist called my new state of mind "clinical burnout." She explained that once my mind and body hit that stage, there was little I could do except to stop and rest. I had become Alice through the looking glass. After all these years, my life was still at the mercy of men, and that realization was terrifying.

I was stripped bare emotionally, mentally, and financially. Ground zero found me selling everything to the highest bidder in order to pay bills. Beautiful books I had collected over my life, DVDs, gold jewelry, clothing, electronics, and any furniture worth something was sold. I saved only a few things: a high-top kitchen table, our bed frames, and several boxes of sentimental items and family photos that represented years of memories we made. And there was one small plastic container that held Savannah's baby things from her first tooth and lock of hair to her baby book and vaccination records. All of it was in a storage unit across town for twenty-five dollars a month. Sometimes I would go sit in the storage unit to sift through Savannah's baby things until my strength returned.

Whatever I was feeling in this moment, I knew my daughter was feeling it more. She was the one who had to walk down the hallways of this affluent middle school jammed with rich teenagers who knew she was the poor kid with no home. Being a thirteen-year-old girl who was homeless, whose mother was borrowing a friend's car, whose mother couldn't get a job or even an interview was a prison in and of itself.

"No one made fun of you at school, did they?" I asked, hoping she hadn't endured any teasing.

"Nope, no one said anything." She smiled at me as she got her books out of her backpack.

During these trials, it was women who came to the rescue. Other mothers, Savannah's girlfriends, and my remaining girlfriends picked us up and placed us on safe ground. They gave us a home (a finished basement) and a car (for six months). They helped me with job leads and shared rides and laundry and life. My one girlfriend, Ms. Gamer, Venmoed me

156

twenty dollars for gas one time so I could get Savannah to and from volleyball practice.

Savannah's friends stood by her at school. She was lucky that they threw her a lifeline instead of an anchor, and I was lucky that Savannah showed me mercy instead of resentment.

I only saw her cry once. We were in the small kitchen of the finished basement in her friend's home, and I was trying to cook pasta on the tiny, portable, camping stovetop. I looked at her and said, "I'm so sorry for all of this. But I promise I will get us out of this, okay?" Tears lit up my eyes. She nodded as her own tears flowed, recognizing the sheer darkness of the situation but also the light of hope I was trying to bring her.

Two days later, the company locked up my storage unit for nonpayment. All my remaining things, including precious photos, the last few pieces of furniture I had, and Savannah's baby things were gone. I lost everything I had to my name.

But I would not fail her. I couldn't. I had promised. And I always kept my promises to Savannah.

Within a few months, I had gotten my substitute teacher license, and started coaching middle school volleyball. I had also been accepted into the MFA Creative Writing program at Ashland University. My confidence returned as I found myself surrounded by people who understood my fight. So, I let go of those people who didn't want to be there and grabbed for dear life onto the people who did.

Ralph Waldo Emerson wrote in *Self Reliance,* "What I must do, is all that concerns me, not what the people think." That's one of my favorite quotes in the essay, although I had failed at living up to its stature. The truth was that I had always cared—deeply—about what people thought of me. When they fled like cockroaches at the first sign of trouble in my life, I'll admit I was hurt.

Within a year's time, I had gone from someone everyone wanted to know to someone no one wanted to touch. A princess to a pauper in record time. The female friendships I had built were hit or miss when it came to support, and it felt truly horrible to be ostracized by some of the women whom I so deeply admired then and now. The change in my status caused a divide that was palpable.

Instead, it was the Upper Arlington mothers, who understood what it meant to give my daughter the education she needed, who swooped in and saved my life.

They saved me so I could save Savannah's life.

I was grateful to them and to my child. Savannah taught me the most while we suffered in the valley. Through all of it, she still believed in me. I don't know why I ever searched for that belief from Sandalwood or anyone else when it had been right there in my daughter's eyes the whole time. She believed me when I told her I would get us out of this, when I said I would keep my promise, when I said the education she was getting would take her places, and when I said I would not let her down. The same eyes that stared at me on the day she was born were staring at me now.

Who are you, Mom?

I had become a woman who would not play nice any longer. What had it ever gotten me to stand idly by and let entitled men control me? This fight lit a fire inside of me. For the first time in years, I was renewed with strength. And in the valley of my immeasurable pain, I found the solid rock foundation to fight from.

Before my collapse, I had searched high and low in all the things the world told me I needed—beauty, thinness, romantic relationships, and moving up the ladder for more money and prestige. But none of those things gave me the happiness, let alone the joy, I was looking for. What I desperately wanted was connection to others, but I was hopelessly disconnected and had been for most of my life. Any happiness I sought, any connection, had always been elusive.

My body itself, so much larger than other girls right from the start, caused a disconnect with both men and women. Later, it was my personality, which was once described as "more like a dude than a chick" because I was so direct, assertive, and ambitious.

I was also suffering from the chronic isolation born out of being misunderstood (an introverted writer), endlessly bullied for my body (fat or thin), and having an opinion while being a woman (a punishable offense). I was a black sheep. An outsider. Eventually, I became more comfortable living on the periphery of the society that wanted me to blend into the background like a Stepford wife. But I couldn't and I wouldn't. There had never been anything about me, physically or otherwise, that allowed me to simply blend in.

Now I could clearly see the advantage of walking away from the things and the people that didn't make sense in favor of the life intended for me. A life that was not meant to toe the line. So, I joined the misfit toys in the ostracized zone and was at peace.

No matter how hard the world pushed, I would not obey. It was simply not in me to do so, and it never had been. I was finally standing on my own two feet, ready to burn it all down.

The match was lit, and we were ready to move on from the rubble.

Chapter 17
Riverside Drive

For the first time in six months, Savannah and I could give people an address that belonged to us. I didn't realize how precious a gift it truly was until I lost it and had to fight to get it back again.

This time, I chose an apartment with a more reasonable budget that was still in the Upper Arlington school district. Our very small two-bedroom apartment with big windows and a broken elevator was on the fourth floor. You would think carrying grocery bags filled with canned soup up four flights of stairs would get easier as time went by, but it never did. It didn't matter.

This new place, it was both quiet and noisy, warm and cool, small and large. The apartment was nestled in a cove of trees right next to the Scioto River with downtown Columbus just five miles from my doorstep. Somehow, I had finally managed to take the duality of my mind and turn it into a real, physical location where my country roots surrounded me and my wandering wings could fly away to the city I loved. Although there was no furniture and nothing hung on the walls, it felt like home. My home.

As I looked around at the emptiness, I realized how very little material things mean. I didn't understand how trivial all that extra stuff was until I came face-to-face with true poverty, homelessness, repossession, and hunger. Even heirlooms meant very little in the face of losing everything I owned. Soon enough, I learned to live without the things everyone claims are necessary and appreciated the things that genuinely are necessary.

Our lives, so mangled the year before, were being rebuilt with a sense of peace and calm restored to them. I was starting to feel good again, too. A miracle in and of itself. My anxiety eased. My depression lifted. My confidence had returned. I had a desire to eat healthier and be healthier. The more energy I dedicated to just simply recognizing who and what I was, the calmer I became in my soul. I was at peace with the path I was on. No small feat.

The first night in our new digs, I slept with a newfound serenity on the couch in my living room. My bedroom, with its two large windows, was too cold. I was exhausted from moving, as was my brother and his bad back, my sister-in-law, my mom, my auntie, Savannah's good friend, and her mother. I slipped on my headphones, ready to drift into my imagination as I had a million times before, looking for answers in some invented world.

But this time, I couldn't relax into it. What an odd occurrence. My imagination was my second home—sometimes my first—where I was always able to create the world I needed or wanted. Frustrated, I put aside the music. Instead, I listened to the sounds of the life I was living.

Large and small jet planes roared over us going to and from the airport. The traffic on the major road just outside our windows included thunderous motorcycles and oversized trucks barreling down the highway. Birds chirping at the other window clashed in direct contradiction to the manmade sounds. Their songs announced the nature just on the other side, where trees and the Scioto River made a home for small animals and dogs and frisbee parks. This new world was alive with the sound of the living.

I had two choices when I was laid bare in the valley: lie in the pit or dig myself out. I chose to fight for my life and for a better life for my kid. One that was authentic even if it wasn't perfect. Don't we all want authenticity in ourselves and the people around us? Rich or poor, thin or fat, pretty or unique, tall or short, male or female, straight or queer. No matter where we start or where we end up, we just want to be allowed to be ourselves. I had to go through the fire to get it, but I earned the right to say, "This is my life and no one else's."

My journey inspired me to name my production company Eleven One Productions. In addition to writing, I was now trying my hand at filmmaking, an expensive undertaking I wasn't financially prepared for, but I was learning. And I had faith I would get there. My company's name reflected that faith. It came from the Bible, specifically Hebrews 11:1, "Now faith is the substance of things hoped for, the evidence of things not seen."

There's a reason it's called a leap of faith. The gap between where you leap from and where you land is where faith lives. It's somewhere between the future you envision and the reality you know to be true. It's the substance of the abstract thoughts we have about the things we believe in. When there is no tangible thing to touch, faith is the stuff that keeps us going.

It seemed like I was surviving by faith alone. It was getting me through every day, the same as water and air and writing and Savannah.

Sometimes that faith was in people. Mr. Sandalwood was back. This time I had initiated it. I was working on a project for my master's degree and needed his expertise, which he offered without strings. The same joy and attraction that had bound us together made its way back into our lives again.

On the phone, he said, "I'm so happy to hear your voice."

"Me too," I said. And I was. The shock of lightning to my system, just from his voice, lifted my spirits at a time when I really needed it. He gave me everything I wanted and asked for: his time, his thoughts, and even his money for the project. If I ever thought he didn't care about me, his actions now spoke otherwise. He was there for me, and anytime I needed him, he made himself available.

What was this thing between us that never seemed to fully go away? I wasn't sure, but I was glad to have him back in my life and to see our spark was still very much alive.

I thought of him fondly as I sat in my new apartment and exhaled relief. I looked around. I was grateful for my new beginning. The foundation was built by the people who were still by my side from Mr. Politico and Ms. Gamer, to Genevieve and my Upper Arlington mothers. I took a deep breath and let myself feel this moment.

I had promised my daughter when she was born, and again in the middle of our trials, that I would make it right. I was doing just that.

I would always make it right for Savannah.

Chapter 18
Tits Up

To take the next steps forward, I would need gumption. Because God knew, and now so did I, that the patriarchy (as a system, not as an indictment of all men) did not want a woman like me in its midst. And neither did Mr. Sandalwood.

As quickly as he had come into my life, a year later he was gone once again. Forgetting to mention he was engaged to someone else was an interesting twist to the situation, but not nearly as interesting as him basically telling me to fuck off when I had the audacity—gasp!—to confront him about it. (He didn't really say fuck off. He would never say that to me, but the sentiment was certainly to fuck right off.) And by now, of course, I was fully in touch with my feminist anger and ready to do something about it. I had become one of *those* women and proudly so.

Like so many other women in the world, I was tired of being the only woman in the room or the only woman going head-to-head with entitled men. I was tired of always answering to a man who had yet to be enlightened about gender equality or having my future and/or paycheck rely on one who could care less about equal rights. I was tired of being played by men, in the bedroom and the boardroom.

I was tired of saying it wasn't all men but rarely coming across the men who "weren't all men," because they were on the sidelines of this war and silently opposed to what was happening instead of taking action to correct it. They wouldn't treat me badly, but they wouldn't stop another man from treating me badly, either. The leaders I wanted to work for, who got it, who valued women, and who wanted them to succeed, those men were few and far between. And, of course, rare was the sighting of a female running things.

I needed to rally, dammit. And that would require gumption. A shit ton of it.

Gumption is something every woman should have. There should be a class taught on it. And that class should be part of every school curriculum, and every girl should be required to take it. To be clear, gumption doesn't make women popular. But the finest women I know with the finest sense of self-worth carry it by the bucket full. They have opinions—how dare they! And they express them—cries of disbelief! And they don't apologize for them—perish the thought!

There is a "Well-behaved women rarely make history" magnet on my fridge, straight from the heart of New York City. I feel like Amy Sherman-Palladino was thinking this very thing when she crafted the lead female roles on *The Marvelous Mrs. Maisel*. Midge, played by Rachel Brosnahan, and the always-incredible Susie, played by the brilliant Alex Borstein, are not well-behaved women. The two famously say, "Tits up!" when the titular character steps on stage to do her (usually illegal) stand-up comedy in the 1950s and 60s.

I raise my eyebrow and put my tits up in salute to every woman who has ever harnessed her gumption and made history. The Rosa Parks and Sheryl Sandburgs and Gloria Steinhams and Condaleeza Rices and Ruth Bader Ginsbergs (RIP RBG) and Marilyn Monroes and Princess Dianas and all the other women who walked around with their gumption worn proudly on their sleeves, refusing to be well-behaved girls sitting quietly in the back of the bus.

I used to sit quietly in the back of the car as a child. My mama still tells stories about how she and my brother would watch me in the backseat. I always had a conversation going with someone or something in my head, but always quietly.

Once I turned thirteen, a switch flipped, and I haven't shut up since, much to the chagrin of many people who know me. Then journalism really lit my fire because, in that world, whether you're male or female is irrelevant. You must be able to talk. And not only that, you have to use your big girl words to speak for those who cannot speak for themselves. As a reporter, I was lauded for not shutting up. What a refreshing notion. Journalism killed the good girl inside me and birthed my gumption, my voice, and my inner feminist.

Tits up, indeed!

During my years in journalism and storytelling, I noticed that just asking a simple question was enough to get people riled up (no matter how nicely I asked it). How dare you even ask the question, let alone actually write something about it. The more gumption I got, the more people wanted to shut me up. Elected officials, heads of corporations, people who had things to hide, exes with secret fiancés, Mr. Glib, and men in high places who put me on blacklists throughout Columbus.

Well, forget those guys.

I am not a well-behaved woman. Dogs are well-behaved. I don't bark, sit, or stay put on command. Finding my gumption and my voice took me a long time, but once I found it, I never did anything on command ever again.

Gumption.

That word has, literally, been stuck to numerous refrigerators with a variety of magnets in a variety of colors, shapes, and sizes, my entire life. I carry that word with me everywhere I go.

I am not demure or quiet. I am an opinionated and bawdy woman. And I like opinionated, bawdy women who don't act like women because they act human. They've got gumption. Their tits are up. Way up. And they like them there.

If you're at all curious about the definition of the word gumption, I'll tell you it's got multiple official and unofficial descriptions, just ask the

Googles. There are a few words and a couple sentences associated with it, but basically, gumption is defined as being a bad ass. It's about being spirited and having the courage and the guts to do and say the things that need to be done and said.

Women cannot make history without gumption. And that includes you.

Tits up, ladies. It's time to rally.

Chapter 19
My Daughter is Sick

When Savannah was fourteen years old, she got the flu and never got better.

For three months, I watched her shrink down to bone thin. I called the doctor, and the doctor said it was nothing. I called again a month later, and she said the same thing. Then I talked to Savannah's father, and we started watching her for bulimia and anorexia nervosa. She swore she did not have an eating disorder, but she kept getting thinner. So, I called the doctor a third time a month after that, and still they did nothing. Allergy, they said. The flu hasn't gone away yet, they said. Teenagers, they said.

On Memorial Day weekend of 2017, my mom called me and said, "She's down to one hundred and sixteen pounds."

On her five-foot eight frame, 116 pounds made her skeletal. "I'm coming to get her."

I took her straight to the emergency room. I was tired of being told that nothing was wrong when I could clearly see that something was very wrong. She was eating everything in the house, and still losing weight at a rapid pace. Losing thirty-six pounds in twelve weeks made her lethargic with constant brain fog. She was pale, and her bones were sticking out.

"We should have her out shortly," the resident doc said. "Teenagers." He winked.

171

That's about the time I went tits up on him. Gumption, baby. I was tired of medical professionals telling me that their fancy degrees meant they knew more about my daughter than I did. I was the one who had nursed her colds, held her head when she vomited, watched her eat and drink, bandaged her scrapes, and kissed away her pain. So, I knew that this illness, whatever it was, wasn't because she still had the flu or because she was a teenager. She was sick, dammit. And by God, they were going to tell me why.

"Listen," I said to him as I slammed my hand down on the bed. Both he and the female nurse turned and looked at me. "Something is wrong with my daughter. And I am not leaving this emergency room until you tell me what it is. So run every blood, urine, and bodily fluid test you have to until you figure what it is."

He paused for a moment. I could see that he was considering arguing with me, but then I think he realized it was pointless. He relented and said, "Okay." He left the room to order the tests. When he did, the nurse handed me the urine sample container with a grin and said, "Good for you." She left the room with a bit of swagger as if my actions emboldened her, too.

My daughter just lay there looking miserable. She was sick but unable to explain it or make it go away or to feel normal. When the nurse came back twenty minutes later and put an IV in her

172

arm, she started to cry. I think she saw my face and knew that there was a diagnosis coming. They're not going to hook you up to an IV unless they were going to put something in that IV.

Thirty minutes after that, the supervising physician came in with the endocrinology doctor who was on call that night. The supervising physician gave us the diagnosis: Type 1 diabetes.

"Honestly," she said, "we can't believe your daughter isn't in a coma right now." Her blood sugar was over six hundred, and apparently that was bad. I didn't know anything about diabetes or its symptoms because it didn't run on my side of the family.

She also was diagnosed with celiac disease with the highest number they'd ever seen. According to her doctor, this condition had likely stunted her growth. (She was five foot eight but should have been five foot ten.) It also contributed to her fatigue and brain fog because the nutrients from her food weren't getting absorbed into her body let alone her brain. And it explained her iron deficiency, which is why she was pale and drawn. The weight loss was because her pancreas had stopped working, so her body had been in keto acidosis for at least three months.

We spent three days in the hospital, where my daughter was poked and prodded and taught how to inject insulin into herself. The roller coaster ride of her blood sugar levels was closely monitored while they tried to stabilize her. We didn't care. We were so relieved to have a diagnosis. A million dollars couldn't make up for confirming that she was in fact sick, knowing why she was sick, and that there was something we could do about it.

The days, months, and two years that followed that diagnosis were a fog for both of us. My daughter had needle marks all over her body from insulin injections and checking her blood sugar constantly. We were exhausted all the time as we tried to stabilize her insulin daily, which was a constantly moving target because her pancreas was fighting to stabilize itself and her body. There were the skin disorders and the huge lumps from unknown reactions. There were the highs that brought on personality changes and the lows that left her feeling out of it.

There were stacks of bills from the constant trips to the emergency room for the new symptoms in addition to the doctor's trips that felt never-ending. The gluten-free diet doubled an already stretched-thin grocery bill. When I lost my job because I was balancing all of this plus getting my master's degree, I just sighed in disbelief.

It was a man who fired me, of course. He had never been a single parent trying to make it work while dealing with a newly diagnosed chronic illness, so he had very little compassion for what we were going through. His actions were deplorable, but I had no energy to fight him. I was too tired to fight it, or even be angry about it. I had to be focused on

Savannah and getting her well. Which we did, eventually, and she was a new person once the fog of her illness lifted.

But her strength and perseverance meant little to some individuals in her life. It was a male coach who told my daughter that while she was "so much better, there was still no place for her" on the team. Because her gumption and her work ethic and her character were less important than him having a winning season (which he didn't have anyway).

My God, what are we teaching our daughters?

By now, Savannah and I were well-versed in hard knocks, but we didn't feel sorry for ourselves. There was no need for that. We looked for the bright spots, we found our tribe of people who supported us, and we just kept putting one foot in front of the other. And I was grateful that she could, because if I hadn't taken her to the ER, who knows what would have happened. If I hadn't spoken up that day, it's possible we would have been discharged from the ER without a diagnosis and within a few weeks she would have collapsed into a coma or worse.

But in that moment, in the ER, I trusted myself more than I trusted the doctor. I wasn't about to take a chance with my daughter's life. I didn't care who I offended or who thought I was crazy or what man was going to call me a bitch for being so assertive. None of it mattered. I knew my daughter was sick, and no one was going to stop me from getting her what she needed.

We, as women, are often taught to ignore our gut in favor of societal niceties. Smile. Be nice. Be polite. Say the right thing. Do the right thing. Respect authority. Do what the doctor says. It's tempting to leave our fate and the fate of the ones we love in someone else's hands and ignore our own instincts. But there are times when that match in the center of our being sparks to life, and it's enough to light us on fire and move us into action. For me, forcing the doctor's hand to take care of my daughter was what had to be done to save her life.

It wouldn't be the last time I had her life in my hands.

Chapter 20
T-Swift Anxiety

I was going to take Savannah to Taylor Swift's *Reputation* concert even if it killed me. We had missed the concert in Columbus because she had been at her dad's house that weekend. So, we got tickets for the following weekend in Pittsburgh. By this point, my anxiety, which was more of a borderline panic disorder, was mostly under control. But I was having terrible flare-ups. Driving to Pittsburgh, going to a concert with a ton of people, being out at night during a thunderstorm, and staying at a hotel in another town was exacerbating my ever-present condition.

By now I recognized that I could not outrun or change the things that had been biologically bestowed on me. They were the reason I had limited my life in many ways. But I fought every day for them to not limit Savannah's. I hid it every chance I could.

Sometimes I would pretend I was tired so another parent would drop Savannah off at night because I had such terrible anxiety going out in the evenings. I limited our vacations and trips to places that I could drive to because I couldn't get on an airplane. I'd busy myself during thunderstorms, telling her I was totally fine, even though my heart was racing so fast I could barely catch my breath.

177

I could have backed out of the concert, too. I could have made an excuse. Lying again would be easy. But I really wanted to take her, and I really wanted to go too. Anxiety didn't kill my desire to do things; it killed my ability to pursue my desires.

I promised myself that I would never burden my daughter with my struggles. I swore I would never pass along my fears through my behaviors. If she came to develop anxieties about things, whether situational or biological, we would deal with it. But I was not going to cause them to grow inside of her simply because they lived inside of me.

As we packed our bags, we blasted Taylor Swift songs and let the excitement fill our bodies. We sang and danced in the living room as we threw the bags toward the door. After grabbing some water bottles and snacks, we packed the car and away we went.

Somewhere around St. Clairsville, Ohio, my heart started tripping and my palms started sweating. I could barely breathe. Savannah was jabbering away, looking at her phone and jamming to the music while I was just trying to hold on. Fear took over every part of my body as I started to breathe harder and faster.

I sang anyway. I laughed and talked and pretended like it was all okay, but inside I was a wreck.

How am I going to make it through this concert?

We checked into the hotel and grabbed our things for the concert, then drove into downtown Pittsburgh to the Heinz Field stadium. After we parked, I could feel my anxiety ticking back up among an adorable crowd of mothers and daughters, sisters and friends. I wanted to enjoy the moment the way everyone else was, but my roaming eyeballs wouldn't stop looking for exits and taking note of all the ambulances and first responders in the crowd. Instead of scrolling the weather map and worrying about the approaching thunderstorm, I tried to take pictures instead.

I was desperate to be in the moment, but I was struggling to stay there. I kept flitting in and out of the memories we were making, jumping from one anxious thought to the next and living my life in between them. Savannah was happy, so I shut my mouth. I kept my anxiety under wraps, but it came out in other ways. Sticking to a schedule and yelling at her when we would veer off it or snapping at little things that I normally wouldn't. It didn't ruin the evening, but it didn't help.

Finally, the music began, and we had the best time. All was forgotten when the concert wands lit up to the beat of the music, and her face was wide open with happiness from her eyes to her smile. We sang at the top of our lungs until our throats hurt and waved our hands until our shoulders failed us. I had dished out a little extra to get our seats as close to the center as possible so that when Swift stood singing

179

almost right in front of us, Savannah screamed with joy. We had pictures and T-shirts and posters and memories. The only thing Savannah didn't have was any memory of my anxiety. She had no idea.

Thank God.

The next day, we drove back home to Columbus, and she slept most of the way. I glanced at her every now and then and breathed a sigh of relief. I had not passed along my anxiety by showing it to her, but I couldn't guarantee her genetics wouldn't cause it to show up later. I could leave the town I came from, but I could not stop biology. I could only pray that if depression or anxiety did show up, my experience would enable me to help her through it.

Chapter 21
Generational Angst

On the fourth of July, my sixteen-year-old daughter was with her friends and her boyfriend. He sent me a text that I had to read a few times.

"Savannah is talking about killing herself."

I knew there was a possibility that changing her birth control was going to affect her emotions, but I didn't realize it might be this bad. Everything she felt was intensified to the point that she thought she couldn't handle her feelings unless she was dead.

As a parent, I spiraled for a second and my thoughts bounced around. First, I was grateful for the boyfriend who had the smarts to let me know. Second, my poor, sweet girl. Third, having been through these emotions myself, I knew I needed to intervene and protect her, but how? Fourth, how did she get to this point? And fifth, where was the fucking parent manual?

Breathe, Steph. Just breathe. Make sure she's safe, and believe her when she says she's hurting.

I called her and asked her to come home immediately. When she got there, I told her what I knew and opened the conversation without judgment, telling her I believed her when she said that she was in pain and that I wanted to help. I kept my emotions in check and our conversations clinical. If I reacted or was emotional, then my daughter would have no structure or safe place to rest in. I was stoic in every interaction so I could guide the ship.

After talking at length, and I could see that, while she was upset, she was not suicidal. And, yes, her birth control was out of whack, but there was more happening inside her than just the hormonal imbalance. I shared my own struggles with anxiety and depression, explaining that I could relate, which helped a lot. She asked me lots of questions and I answered them honestly. One thing was clear, there was more to this situation than just her hormones being out of whack.

She needs help, Steph.

My daughter needed to speak with someone, that much was obvious. She was bewildered by the roller coaster ride of first love, the hormonal changes of new medications, and the family dynamics that were suddenly causing her pain and frustration. She didn't know how to handle the surging emotions inside of her. I told her she was strong enough to find out what was ailing her and face it. Maybe that would require medications, maybe it wouldn't, but she most certainly needed a licensed professional to help guide her through it.

You might be the problem, Steph.

I winced at the notion. But after everything we'd been through, it was a distinct possibility. It's hard to accept that as a parent I could cause my child's pain, but it was essential to understand how I might have played a part in what was happening to her. I opened myself up to this possibility. I told Savannah it was okay if I was part of the problem and that I would help fix it.

You need to call someone right now, Steph.

I immediately called Nationwide Children's Behavioral Center and got her an appointment. She went in within a few days and started her therapy sessions. Because she was sixteen, I went with her the first time. But after that, she went alone so that she could talk freely about what was hurting her without consequence or judgment.

Does she need medication?

The psychologist believed that Savannah didn't need any medications to help her through this period. She said that everything that was ailing my child stemmed from environmental triggers. Her diabetes diagnosis, the birth control change, her first boyfriend, and other circumstances outside of our home, were primarily driving her emotions.

Okay, how do we get her through this?

The number one issue her psychologist discussed was that Savannah needed to learn better coping methods. Mostly, she had to learn how to set emotional and physical boundaries with people in order to protect herself. She had to learn how to speak up and confront difficult situations. By nature, she was shy and reserved with a heart for pleasing people. The psychologist helped her move beyond these traits in order to be secure in, and please, herself.

And what about those environmental triggers?

Savannah had to learn that taking care of herself first was more important than pleasing anyone else in her life. This was, of course, the hard part because it involved possibly disappointing the people she loved dearly. She wouldn't be able to change their behaviors, but she could change her own and create space for herself by setting boundaries in her relationships. It was a hard lesson to learn at sixteen.

After about three months of therapy and practicing her behavioral exercises (as well as adjusting to the new birth control medication), my daughter felt strong enough to leave therapy. She felt far more prepared to handle her emotional life after getting the strategies she needed to cope.

The mental health playbook for kids is not simple for many parents. Some issues require one or many medications, years of therapy, and/or other cognitive, behavioral, or psychiatric measures. There is no manual to tell parents how to support a child in crisis. But the one thing all parents should do is believe a child who says they're in pain, then get them the help they need.

I knew I did the right thing for my daughter in this moment, but what if it happened again? Had I given her enough to make sure she could cope with life moving forward? It was my job to watch out for her as a child, but once she was an adult, she'd have to find these solutions for herself.

Did I do enough?

I hoped I had. And that's about the time the #MeToo movement took off.

Chapter 22
#MeToo On Fire

A very cold reality was starting to take shape around me. I could speak and fight and change and give my daughter every possible advantage, but until the world changed, my daughter would still have to pick up the sword and fight for her place in a society that continued to believe women were second-class citizens. To say that I was grateful when activist Tarana Burke started the #MeToo movement was an understatement, because, yeah, me too.

I watched in real time with my daughter how the #MeToo movement began to tear down walls that had long existed for women. Unfortunately, it took multiple reports of seemingly good guys assaulting women for the change to really take hold. But those stories presented an opportunity for me to open a conversation with my daughter about women's rights that helped us reshape the way we viewed the world and the way we consumed it.

One of the consumables we discussed was the good old-fashioned fairy tale. The princess fairy tale, in all its versions, is so ubiquitous that it has been engrained into the hearts and minds of women everywhere. These stories create unrealistic expectations which guide our culture and, ultimately, create emotional and mental distress for women (and many men) on a global level.

Fairy tales are presented as though that's how real-life works. Except it doesn't. By the time I sat down with my daughter to discuss it, I had two very good friends who had been raped, I had dealt with two assaults, and I had seen the wreckage in other women's lives that were then magnified by the #MeToo movement. To be clear, I don't blame fairy tales exclusively—can we talk about fashion dolls and the Barbie influence?—but I had to question the pervasive and persistent story lines of women existing only for the pleasure of men.

Consider the fairy tale of a lovely mermaid who's cursed by a mean, old witch (note the undertone of a young women versus an old woman) and loses her voice just before she meets her prince. He only needs to kiss her, and they will live happily ever after. As a child, this was delightful. But as an adult with a teenage daughter, I read that fairy tale again and a new, dangerous storyline emerged that was about taking advantage of a girl who couldn't speak. It was saying that the prince should kiss the girl even though she could not verbally consent to the sexual advance.

When you start to break down the underlying messages of fairy tales, you start to see how they negatively impact women (and men). I had to ask the questions: How had I let my daughter indulge in such fairy tales? And how had I indulged in them myself? The subtle message of sexual assault—the idea that a man had not only the right to

187

kiss her but that her very voice depended upon his getting a kiss—was so interwoven into the norms of our society and the way we view fairy tales that it was invisible to me.

Suddenly, images flashed in my head of girls being silenced by a hand clamped across their lips or tape over their mouths, or the intangible silencing imposed by the threat of beatings, abuse, rape, and death. And then only being released from that state by the hands of a man. How had a message this disturbing become such an ever-present part of culture? As women, how had we let it?

Sure, lots of little girls love playing princess, and I understand its appeal. I have three princess crowns in my home to prove it. (They are my crowns, mind you, not my daughter's.) I love the idea of being a princess because I love the idea of having wealth, fashion (I want Kate Middleton's entire wardrobe), and power. I got up early to watch Diana become a princess. I watched the documentary about Megan Markle (mostly in horror of the way she was treated, but in awe of the change she's focused on bringing to the world). I love the idea of being in a position of power to help people and to change the way society works for the better. But to be clear, my love of being a princess has nothing to do with a man.

Why, then, do all fairy tales insist on it? Why do they insist female silence is imperative to success and love? Why do they pit women against

188

each other, particularly young versus old? Why do
they teach little girls that their voice can only be
released by a man? Or that the only way to unlock
potential in their lives is for a man to come along
with the key? Or that Stockholm syndrome (where a
beast holds a beauty captive) is what they should be
wishing for? Or that getting married to a prince is the
only dream to be cherished (in stories about a Cinder
girl locked away by an evil stepmother)?

A brilliant article by Jeff Guo featured in the
January 25, 2016, issue of *The Washington Post*
pointed out how Disney princesses and their
respective films were both mirroring culture and
shaping it in ways that could be detrimental to the
young girls watching them, particularly around the
issue of voice.

For example, according to Guo, *The Little
Mermaid* "sparked a trend in Disney princess films
where women spoke three times less than men in the
films." The data, he reported, came from a 2016
capstone project that linguists Carmen Fought and
Karen Eisenhauer researched and presented to several
audiences titled "A Quantitative Analysis of
Gendered Compliments in Disney Princess Films."
The project analyzed dialogue from the Disney
princess franchise. The results showed that *The Little
Mermaid* and almost every princess movie thereafter
(with the exception of *Brave*) had men speaking more
than 50 percent of each movie, drowning out
women's voices by sometimes large margins.

189

Their report said that men spoke 68 percent of the time in *The Little Mermaid*, 71 percent of the time in *Beauty and the Beast*, and a whopping 90 percent of the time in *Aladdin*. Even *Frozen*, which had a much more promising ending than the princess movies before it, had men speaking 59 percent of the time.

Guo reported that the most noticeable positive trend was that the modern princesses tended to be complimented more on their traits than their looks. He attributed much of the shift in moving away from looks to the fact that *Brave* and *Frozen* were conceived, written, and directed by women. How very refreshing that a Disney princess was created by someone of the same gender.

To date, the only princess movie I can tolerate is *Ever After: A Cinderella Story* starring Drew Barrymore. I do like Anne Hathaway's take on *The Princess Diaries*. And the Camila Cabella-led *Cinderella* isn't so bad, either. I was glad to see Billy Porter rocking his gender-fluid look in fabulous heels as a fairy godmother. His activism and gender expression through fashion was a right he had to fight for, and that we all benefit from.

Author and feminist Rebecca Solnit started a new type of princess story with *Cinderella Liberator*. In Solnit's version, Cinderella is known as simply Ella. She doesn't marry the prince. He's her good friend. And no one saves her. She learns she is strong enough to not only save herself but others by standing up for what she believes in.

What I wouldn't give for an animation studio to grab hold of Solnit's version. They could begin to counter the weight of the Disney franchise and its throat hold on our perception of a certain type of princesses as portrayed through the male gaze.

The male gaze is a term first coined by filmmaker and theorist Laura Mulvey in an academic paper she wrote in 1973 titled "Visual Pleasure and Narrative Cinema." It was then published two years later in *Screen* magazine.

You'll find many different explanations of the theory on the Googles, but it essentially means seeing everything from a straight man's perspective. More specifically, the theory asserts that the media and arts culture—particularly film—assume the intended audience member is a heterosexual male. As a result, women are only presented and viewed in a way that caters to this audience, so women are usually portrayed as passive objects and often objectified sexually.

Examples of this might be a camera's slow pan up or down a woman's body; or when women are dressed inappropriately in tight, uncomfortable clothing while men in the same situation are dressed in comfortable, appropriate attire; or when a female character is only defined by her relationship to a man; or when women's voices are secondary to a man's or nonexistent.

191

A famous cliché of this masculine perspective in movies is when a female lead will turn to the man and say, "What do we do now?" As if a woman has no ability to come up with ideas on her own and must turn to the man for guidance. If you don't believe me, just watch twenty action movies prior to #MeToo with male and female leads. At some point in that movie, the perfectly capable, badass woman will turn to the man and say, "What do we do?"

In short, the male gaze assumes audience. Men are the primary directors, producers, and distributors of movies, so the product is designed by and for them. Including our beloved princesses.

Thinking outside the box isn't hard. For example, who says a princess must be a woman at all? I know plenty of men who would really enjoy that crown and some fabulous high heels. And who says the prince must be a man? Why can't it be an enviably fabulous lesbian? And who says the princess needs a prince at all? Maybe the princess wants to go on adventures and rule the kingdom by herself. Why are we still creating any film or media that is presumed to be only viewed through the eyes of men?

This perspective is also destructive to men. The toxicity it creates in men is grotesque. I would argue that Laura Mulvey's brilliant theory didn't go far enough. The dominant male paradigm hurts men too because it only represents a white, athletic, able-bodied, cis-gender, attractive, tall, straight male standard that few men can attain.

We are told in thousands of subtle ways every day that the only worthy type of male is the white, athletic, straight one. Men are not allowed to live outside of the male gaze either. They are not allowed to feel anything or do anything outside of what that paradigm says they should. If they try, they are punished.

What a disservice to men as human beings that they are told they cannot and should not feel or express the full spectrum of human emotions. That raising their children is secondary to their careers. That they must only be strong protectors and providers and nothing else. That loving someone who is anything but the prescribed hot, heterosexual woman is something they should be embarrassed about.

As a teenager, I was sitting in my living room when my brother came in. He was having a side conversation with my mom. Even though I was watching a soap opera, my ears perked up when I heard the word, "fat."

My brother said something along the lines of, "I really like her, but she's fat. What should I do?"

My teenage brother liked a girl who was overweight and felt like he had to question whether that was okay. As though she were a criminal. As though it was a crime to even like her let alone date her. If she were thin, it wouldn't even be a question. But because she was overweight, it required a whole conversation. It required permission, by God.

And it wasn't just my brother, and it wasn't just limited to dating.

Women know what happens when men leave the room. We know that in an office setting, the men leave the room and talk about the woman with big boobs. They go to the bathroom to make deals and inform the women later. We know that men tell us one thing to our face and turn around and tell their friends we're annoying or fat or ugly. We know guys ask permission to date us, hire us, and include us. Maybe not actively or explicitly, but through their actions men ask permission of other men.

When a man's girlfriend meets his friends and those friends look her over, then wink at him and say, "Nice," that is their approval. She doesn't even need to speak. If she looks good, she is good. And every man would be lying if he said he didn't feel a little relief after receiving that stamp of approval. All that behavior falls under the male gaze and the prescriptive way that men are told to behave.

Women know it, and many of us hate it. It's why we have the #MeToo movement and feminism (which should be for women *and* men).

And this was my dilemma now with my daughter. I could write the rules of our house any way I liked, but when she left my home, my daughter was subjected to the rules of a heterosexual, white man's world. So, all that fighting I did, all those swords and daggers I carried, she would have to pick them up, wipe off the blood, and start all over again.

She recognized this dynamic very clearly during an exercise about diversity and inclusion at her high school. My daughter came home that day, irate. Her face flamed red as she slammed down her backpack on the kitchen floor saying, "You are not going to believe this."

She explained how the teachers lined up all the kids on the middle line on the basketball court with everyone facing the same direction and said, "Everyone starts in about the same place when you're born." (Which is not true. I'll get to that.) They proceeded to ask the kids a variety of questions like, "Did you eat dinner last night?" or "Do you always have new shoes to wear?" If they answered yes, they took a step forward. If they answered no, they took a step back.

Savannah said that by the end of it, she was so infuriated she could barely speak. All of the kids at the front of the gym were white males in two-parent homes, and just behind them, were their female counterparts. All of the kids at the middle line or in the back—where my daughter was—were kids of color, kids in low-income families, and kids of single parent homes. They were from families like mine, struggling to give their kids a good education.

"How am I supposed to get ahead when I'm starting so far behind?" she said.

195

Unfortunately, it wouldn't be the last time she would experience her poverty in direct contradiction to her peers' privilege. Just a few months later as she pushed herself to earn a 4.0 GPA while working a near full-time job and battling diabetes, she said again, "These kids, they complain because they got a BMW instead of an Audi. And we can barely put food on the table."

Her frustration was palpable because she had seen so clearly in that exercise that rich white males were ahead of the game. But she was also living in the existential truth that, even though our society assumes we all start in the same place, we don't. "Work hard and you'll get ahead," people say. The reality is that some people must work much, much harder than others. And even then, they don't always catch up.

My daughter was reacting to the truth of the world and feeling trapped by its invisible prison. I understood where she was coming from, but I had no response except to say that an education (formal and informal) would be the key to getting her out of it. Educated women who fight to the top are one solution to the gaze.

"I promise you that the education you're receiving is your ticket out," I said of her high school frustrations. "Stay focused on that and you'll be street smart and book smart. There is power in that."

Later on, I winced thinking about what I had said to her because the truth was, I hoped there was power in that. I had a master's degree, and even though I knew better, I was still trapped by the gaze and all its manifestations. As I lived through the #MeToo movement and all the conjecture that followed, I kept waiting for the moment when what I told my daughter became true. When would the gaze be just a theory and no longer a staple of our society?

How could I explain to my daughter that so long as men controlled the money and the power, the patriarchal system would still control this world? And that my daughter's generation will have to bear that inequality unless my generation can find a way to fix it.

All I could do was promise her that her smarts and her fight for equality would be an important and necessary contribution to the world. It would be a contribution that, someday, would hopefully give her children (if she chooses to have them) a boost beyond what either of us was able to accomplish.

Chapter 23
Gazing West

No one was more surprised than me when I realized that the male gaze was not only the foundation of our society but of my own mind. It had so permeated the media I consumed that it had naturally become a part of my vision.

And now, it had to go. It no longer served me, so there was no longer a place in my life for it.

To start? I had to change my name.

My maiden name was my father's name. My married name was my husband's name. After we divorced, I went back to my maiden name. So, all my life, my name and my identity had come from a man. But I lived a life where I had been emotionally, mentally, and sexually abused at the hands of men. And now that I recognized my own blind spot of the male gaze, I knew I could not move forward with a man's name.

No. My name had to be mine. I had to own it. I had to start from square one if I was going to eradicate the male gaze from my life and replace it with the vision I had for myself. And whatever name I chose, it had to be born of a female in my life not a male. It had to come from my mother.

When I was in my late twenties after Savannah was born and I'd started this journey, my mom bought me a simple silver necklace whose charm was a small compass. The letters N, S, E, W were imprinted on the front, and the phrase, "There are no shortcuts to anywhere worth going," was engraved on the back.

My new last name had to relate to this gift. This simple act of a mother believing in her daughter and trying to help her find her way was what I wanted represented in my new name. The women in my life were always the ones who did the fixing after the men did the breaking. I wanted to honor the women who sustained me, who picked me up along the way, who shared my tears and laughter, and who held my hand.

But mostly, it was my mother. So, to honor her on my path forward after putting myself through a master's program, raising Savannah, and finally finding the path of my life, I used the compass, plus my love of film (which is so prominent on the West coast), to choose West. On September 29, 2020, I gave my testimony to the judge, and she ordered my name changed. At the end of the hearing, she said, "I just love what you're doing here. Have a good day, Ms. West."

I thanked her and went on my way. It took a moment for the emotions on my insides to work their way to my outsides, but when the tears finally made their appearance, a great deal of joy came with them.

My actions had broken a generational chain that society had put there the day I was born—that a man owned me. But when the female judge called me Ms. West, I owned me. I owned my name. I owned who I was, even the imperfect parts. Every single thing I had dreamed for myself and my daughter had reached a meaningful conclusion. In that singular moment I knew I had become my own person, for better or worse.

I no longer felt like a victim of my circumstances and a single mom with little to my name. Instead, I felt like a warrior who was quick on my feet, creative with my resources, and eager to be the best mom possible. I no longer felt the need to take on everything and be everything to everyone. I cared less about making others feel one hundred percent comfortable and more about me being one hundred percent comfortable with who I was. No male gaze required.

This life-changing moment is, of course, when Sandalwood made another appearance in my life. I had sent a group email about a friend of ours, and within an hour, my phone rang. I was in a meeting with my boss and missed the call, so I listened intently to his voicemail. No matter how angry I was at him, I was always happy to hear his voice. My stomach would always flip when I saw his name on my phone.

His voicemail said the secret fiancé was no more, and he was single again. "I miss you," he said. "How are you?" All the same things he always said. All the same joy and all the same feelings. It seemed they would never go away for us. And yet, I could tell that something had changed in me. I could have called him back right then, but I didn't. I didn't want to. I was still pissed, and I didn't want to give him any leeway on this one. So, I created distance by texting instead of calling and wrote something flippant like, "That doesn't surprise me," and waited for his response.

I wanted to get into it with him. I wanted to have the angry conversation because in the past I had made it so easy for him with my softened voice and understanding nature. I didn't want to make it easy this time. Our entire relationship, I had been starry-eyed and tempered. I wanted this conversation to be livid and uncontrolled. I wanted it to feel like it was part of the real world and not some fairy tale. I wanted to passionately let out the pain of this relationship. And when the arguing was done, I wanted to sink into the beautiful, newly created part of our relationship where we saw each other at our worst and still held strong. So, I waited for the squabble. The real talk.

I waited and waited and waited some more.

After a few days, I sent a follow-up text. A week later, I sent another and tried to call. Nothing. And now I was desperate. Desperate for a response. Desperate to hash it out for real. So, I sent another text and another and another. I wrote the pissed off thing in my head that you should never send: "YOU called me and I respond and now you won't respond???" The texts that followed went through the five stages of grief, ending with acceptance when

201

there was still no response. No fight, no nothing, just silence.

I wish I could say this was the first time he had done that, but this was his thing. To block me out of his life in one form or another when it suited him.

I wasn't satisfied with the ending, but I wasn't surprised either. I was just tired. And, surprisingly, okay. For the first time in the last eight years, I didn't try to please him. I tried to fight with him. I tried to assert myself with him. It came out like a bad romantic comedy, I realize, but at least I was going into it ready to stand up for myself. If I ever wondered how he'd handle fighting with me or how he would deal with my ambivalence or my assertiveness or my craziness, I had my answer. He had started something he couldn't finish (again). So, I finished it for him.

Right about the time I sent my last text, Savannah popped into my room and wanted to go get food. That's when something miraculous happened.

I was in the car with my daughter, and we were doing what we always do: talk, talk, talk, play road games, and talk some more. My daughter, now eighteen and hilarious, made a crack off something I said, and I started laughing.

I mean, laughing.

Really laughing.

The sound bubbled up and out of me like champagne on New Year's Eve. Then Savannah started laughing with such a fizzy, effervescence that

202

gushed so quickly and clearly out of her that I couldn't help but laugh some more. And the more I laughed, the more she laughed. And so on, until we were back home with our drinks.

For the first time in my life, I could laugh without reservation. The darkness had abated; the light was renewed. I rejoiced that my daughter had found her laughter and anger and emotions long before I had. She had a voice that was uniquely hers, she used it regularly, and I could not be happier. Hopefully, it would stay with her and serve her well for the rest of her life.

I hope.

I wish.

I wish I'd found my voice sooner.

I wish things would have been different with Sandalwood.

I wish my dad had been a feminist and told the world and its standards to fuck off instead of giving me the middle finger and telling me I had to change to meet his gaze.

I wish my brother had gone out with a girl he said was too fat to date.

I wish there had been more choices for women in my small hometown and in all the small towns across America.

I wish women were paid the same as men and didn't have to work twice as hard to get it.

I wish movies, art, and politics were led by the women whose backs they were built on.

I wish male-dominated workspaces would stop designing hours and requirements through a man's eyes and start designing them through a woman's.

I wish more workspaces were led by women.

How different would this world be if women had a voice and agency in their own lives and in the media representations of their lives?

How different would this world be if women saw themselves through their own lens instead of a man's?

How different we would all be for the clear vision of a woman undisturbed by the male gaze? I was going to find out. With my new name and my gumption fully loaded, I set about showing the world exactly what that looked like. If it took me the rest of my life, I would create change that my daughter could benefit from, even if it was small.

Chapter 24
The Lost COVID Year

After all those years of struggling, it ended up being the NBA's Cleveland Cavaliers who saw through the bullshit and offered me a job in sports.

It was an opportunity more than a year in the making. I was supposed to interview in March of 2020. The day before I left, Mr. NBA, who would be my manager, called to cancel due to the uncertainty surrounding the spread of a new virus that was highly contagious and raging through the United States. The next day, the state of Ohio shut down due to the illness known as COVID-19, caused by the SARS-CoV-2 virus, and the job was frozen. What followed was a nightmare I call the lost COVID year.

After that lost year, the Cavaliers job reopened, and Mr. NBA reached out. I reapplied, interviewed, and waited to hear.

I cannot say enough about the team of people who interviewed me over two months and four rounds of intense meetings that always ended with the feeling that they really wanted me there. They were genuinely interested in diversity, inclusion, and hiring the best people for the job. I felt respected in this role, and it would be an amazing opportunity. After the disappointment of losing the job at the NHL all those years ago, it felt like a huge win to get an offer from the NBA. Especially in a role that, in days past, would have automatically gone to a man. And it was mine for the taking.

I turned them down.

A very good friend of mine, who I lost to breast cancer, once told me that all a woman needs is "just that one opportunity" to turn everything around. That one thing to make the difference at a time when she's hurting for a chance that will get her going again, and bring her back to life.

And like my friend said, this Cavaliers opportunity could bring me to life. Or maybe there was something else.

Once the Cavaliers' offer was in front of me, I realized that the lost COVID year between interviews had changed me in ways I could never have prepared for. Yes, life felt more precious. Yes, I told loved ones how much I loved them. Yes, the overarching themes of mortality pulsed through my body. Yes, it was a good reminder to call my mother more. But it went much further than that for me.

That lost COVID year made me feel like I was living in an invisible prison, and the inmates were running the asylum. It was jarring to go from living in a free country to living in a lockdown. The experience impressed upon me how precious freedom was to me in a way I had never felt before.

As the restrictions eased and society slowly came back to life, I struggled mightily with the idea of confinement. Unlike the dreams I had been chasing pre-COVID, my dream post-COVID was to never have my life confined that way again. Anything that tried to lock me down in a building, schedule, or location, suddenly gave me anxiety. Feeling controlled by any authority brought on a sense of pure panic. And as someone who had always bucked authority, even as a teenager, the new lockdown only exacerbated that personality trait.

In addition to that, Savannah was preparing to graduate high school, and I was going to be on my own again. As a result, I was refocusing my life in a post-COVID world (with all its PTSD and trauma), trying to answer the question, "How do I get to be the person I want to be and not feel like a trapped animal?"

When the Cavaliers offered me the job, I was traumatized, exhausted, lonely, and scared. I wanted to find a way back to the happiness I felt when I was a journalist or making films or raising my daughter or spending time with Sandalwood or almost any moment before the COVID lockdown stole some of my innocence. But it seemed the pathway didn't exist. After years of taking care of everyone around me, I just wanted a moment in the sun where someone was taking care of me in a world that didn't feel so out-of-control.

And in that moment, all I could think of was Sandalwood.

After all these years, he remained a white noise in my head. Everywhere I went, the buzz persisted like a fan on a hot night drowning out the

207

sounds of life itself. In my exhaustion, all I wanted was for him to wrap his arms around me and say that it would all be okay. That he was proud of me and that he was sorry for how it had all unfolded. It was, of course, a fantasy. He was a fantasy, confined to my head, in a permanent state of lockdown.

It pained me that I was still wondering how I would look through his eyes. I hated that I was asking myself what he would think of me if he knew I worked for the Cavaliers. It was a dream job, by any standard, to work for such a famed organization. What would he think if he knew what I'd accomplished? Would this one decision be the thing that would change his mind about me? And just like that, once again, my whole life was teetering on the viewpoint of a man and what he might think of me.

No.

I was not going to make even one more decision thinking of a man. And especially not Sandalwood. I forcibly pushed him to the back of my mind and thought carefully through the decision for myself. Did I want the job? Was I a good fit for this organization? Could I give them one hundred percent given the way I was feeling post-COVID?

I had loved sports from a young age. I remember being on the ball field playing pitcher or catcher to my brother's batting. After that, I played sports myself in volleyball and basketball. My height made me a commodity, and I was a decent athlete. So, would I be a good fit? Yes, I would be great at the job. Would I give one hundred percent? I would give ten thousand percent, everything I had. And I had a strong desire to work for Mr. NBA. He seemed like a great mentor and someone who believed, deeply in his core, in equal rights. That made him unique because that open attitude wasn't always something I had encountered in the world of sports.

But the more I thought about it, the more I kept arriving at the same decision: the timing wasn't right. I was a different person now. The lost COVID year had changed me. During lockdowns and restrictions, I had taken the time to reflect on my life. Looking back, I tried to understand how I'd gotten to this place. And was this the right place?

It became clear that the only thing I had ever loved doing was storytelling in all its forms. Writing. Filmmaking. Communications. Books. In those worlds, I got to tell tales, talk to people, quench my insatiable appetite for knowledge, learn new things, try new things, and meet new people. I was a storyteller. A storyteller who had realized years ago that my beloved field of print journalism was dying, and if I wanted to raise my daughter a certain way, I had to leave journalism and make more money. What followed were years upon years of taking jobs I wasn't passionate about because I needed the money. I'd built a career (sort of) in fields I wasn't interested in but that were adjacent to my love of storytelling and paid me well.

I just couldn't do it anymore.

I realized post-COVID that I had spent my life building things for others in fields that were only mildly interesting to me with people I loved and mentors whom I was grateful for. But now I wanted to build things I loved in a career that I had put on hold to raise my daughter. Even though I wanted to work for the Cavaliers and help them tell their story, I wanted to do my own thing more. I didn't want to feel confined to a life that wasn't authentically me anymore. And if the lost COVID year had taught me anything, it was that life is too short to live in a state of confinement, physically or mentally.

So, I moved forward in a different direction with the hopes that someday I would return to sports and perhaps have an opportunity to work with Mr. NBA again. This stage of my life was about slowing down, taking a beat, and letting myself decompress. I needed to unwind eighteen years of struggle by unpacking the boxes I had so neatly tucked away in my mind in order to make it through every day as a single mom.

I didn't have time to think much while raising Savannah. Everything felt like it was always on fire. My whole life was about having to take the next action, right or wrong, to just keep moving forward. But now it was time to breathe, to sit in my emotions and my mistakes and my successes and let it all come out. I needed to feel the pain, the envy, the anger, the happiness, the laughter, and many more

210

emotions I had filed away under "I'll get back to this when Savannah graduates."

It was all unpacked at my feet. What to do with it? I had grappled with the word "if" across three generations: first my mother and her life, then me and my life, and finally Savannah and her life. Who could my mother have been if someone had encouraged her? Who could I have been if men had not abused me? And finally, who could Savannah be if I made all the right choices? And who would she be if I made the wrong ones? I'd been driven by absolute fear that I would mess her up. That I would cause her to miss out on some aspect of her life if I couldn't get it together in mine.

I wondered, time and again, if the struggle was worth it. But every time Savannah fought for herself and won, every time her character expressed itself, and every time she successfully overcame an obstacle, it reminded me that it was worth it. I had accomplished my goal and given her a different life. She knew, without a doubt, that opportunity existed for her outside her bubble. She also knew that whatever life she dreamed of, I was out there fighting for her to have it.

Through my failures and my successes, I had pulled us out of a world with limited opportunities and moved us to one with possibilities. We were both better for my wins and my losses. Life, as it turns out, is lived in both the sunlight of realization and the shadow of a misconceived notion.

211

Through it all, my faith proved itself stronger than my circumstances, which was unexpected. For the longest time, I felt like I should do it all by myself. I tried to fight the bad stuff with either a pleasing disposition or swinging fists. It had been counterintuitive for me to lean into the pain and absorb it in a constructive way. But pain is necessary. Strength is born in your bones when you embrace it and let it do its work inside you. Pain is a good teacher. Sometimes, it's the only thing that can teach you what you need to know about people, life, and yourself.

I had no idea the strength I had in my body or how far I would go for my daughter to have the same rights, education, and possibilities that a son would have had. That realization changed my life. Now Savannah was eighteen years old and had earned an almost full ride to a top-ranked university after graduating Magna Cum Laude. I no longer felt the same pressures or strains of raising her the way I did when she was four. Or ten. Or fourteen. My daughter would always need me, but the way she needed me had changed again.

Her independence from me was staring me in the face. And I was okay with that. I had given her everything. My time, my love, my life. And I regretted none of it. Lost jobs, lost men, and lost friends were nothing compared to what I had gained. This thoughtful, emotional, smart, resilient, disciplined young woman was filled with character, and I knew she'd be okay.

It was my turn to focus a little more on what my life would mean, what it would be, independent of being defined as Savannah's mom. My wide-open future was filled with possibility. It came back to the same question of, "How do I get to be the person I want to be?"

The answer, like days past, was simple. I didn't know. That brought with it a new kind of fear mixed with a hint of excitement. I was not the same person I was when I walked out my ex-husband's door. I wouldn't get to be a mother again. Maybe I wouldn't find love again. Maybe I would never be any of the things I had dreamed of being. Maybe I would lie down to die wrapped in the comfort of only my fantasies. Or maybe my fantasies would become real. It was scary to teeter between reality and fantasy. I wondered how much time I had left to do the things I wanted to do, feeling lost again in my forties the way I had in my twenties. Without my north star, the path was dark, but I felt I knew which direction to walk. The rest would come to me, step-by-step.

As faith propelled me forward, I paused to look back just once more. In the rearview mirror, I saw my life and realized that what could have been was no longer relevant.

I could no longer question a past that had given me such a beautiful daughter. Raising

Savannah was, by far, the best ride of my life. Sometimes it was too fast or too slow. Sometimes I wanted to be sick on the steep hills. And many times, we had to rely on our wits, our love, our faith, and our sheer determination to get by every day. In our struggle, I found something deeply satisfying in life itself. It felt like we'd earned our life every day. We'd get thrown down a pit and have to claw our way back out, and that was richly rewarding because it was our fight, together.

I can say with absolute certainty, knowing the good and the bad, that I'm so glad I bought the ticket. Savannah had become her own person through a life that gave her more choices than I'd ever had. She was walking into her future confident, excited, and filled with wonder for all the possibilities she had at her fingertips.

And for the first time in my life, so was I.

Epilogue

Dear Savannah,

In a few weeks, you'll leave for college. I can chart the passage of time in your long legs and toothy smile. It seems like all I did was blink, and suddenly, your baby face transformed into a lovely young woman. Your wordless cries have turned into streams of witty and insightful chatting. I've earned some wrinkles and laugh lines. We both have grown, as has my love for you.

During these eighteen years of raising you, I often wonder who has grown more—me or you? Did I teach you how to fly, or was it the other way around? I don't know. But I can say that in these last eighteen years, I have become someone I hope you're proud of someday.

As you grow and age, you'll learn that life isn't always about being great or even good. It's about being brave enough to walk through the fire and help others in the process. I think life is more meaningful when it's spent helping people, animals, the environment—whatever—so long as it's useful. But how you live your life is ultimately up to you.

You will not do life perfectly, kiddo. No one does. Remember that. There is no guidebook or rule book. We all just kind of make it up as we go along. I like to rely on my faith because I've seen a lot of miracles. But you can make up your own mind about that. Your choices are yours.

You will make horrible mistakes. And, hopefully, you will fail a lot because you have tried a lot. Be okay with that. Failure is part of a life well-lived. I should know. I've met failure so many times, it's like an old friend who comes to dinner. But I hope that when you turn the coin of my life over, you can see all my successes, too. I'm your mother, but I'm also human. And I've learned a few lessons that will help you as you enter college.

I can't list them all, but I can pass along the ones I think are most important.

I have loved and been loved. I have let people down, sometimes repeatedly, and I have been let down a lot. I have cried and laughed and had my heart broken. I have broken other people's hearts, including my mother's. That is the worst heart to break, dear daughter. But, at some point, if you want to be your own person, you will have to break mine. Don't be scared to do it when the time comes. I will still love you.

I have been happily married and sadly divorced. Your Dad and I were in love when we made the choice to have you. We love you. And that will never change.

Work is work. It's not your life, unless you're lucky enough to make money doing what you love. In that case, "Bravo, child!" Be poor if it means living your passion. I would much rather have you staying in my basement and following your dreams, than living in a mansion and dying inside. You will have to make that choice someday, like we all do.

Choose wisely.

I have seen the good, the bad, and the ugly. I have been all three.

I know enough to know not to sweat the small stuff. I do it anyway. I hope you don't. It will keep you from being your best. And you have so much good to offer.

Here's what matters: love. What you love, who you love, and how you love. There. You're set for life. Go.

Yes, it really is that simple.

I have a mom who loves me, and I am your mom. I get better at being a daughter and a mother as time moves on. So will you. Parenting is hard. Don't ever give up on it if you choose to have a child. If that's your path, then someday you'll understand why it meant so much to me that I dropped you off at, and picked you up from, school every day until you could drive. I never regretted the irritated coworkers or rushed mornings.

I would have regretted choosing anything else over you.

I have acquaintances, friends, and best friends. I cherish all three. Don't be offended if someone you call a friend thinks of you as an acquaintance. This will happen over and over. Focus on the people who want to be in your life and make the effort to be there. That will make all the difference.

I have desired all different kinds of men. Some of them I've gotten, others not so much. There have been a couple men who got me. But no one has ever had the real me. I wish they had. And you will, too. Be one hundred percent yourself, and you'll get there. Date a lot. And choose a variety of people. You'll be surprised by what really gets your attention. The one that lasts won't be superficial. Beauty is deceptive. Make sure you look twice.

I have loved my body and hated it. I have admired it and cursed it. I have never been at ease with it or just thankful that it worked properly. Be thankful for your body. It is your tool in life. Treat it with respect.

I know I spend too much time wanting the things and talents that belong to other people, instead of spending time appreciating my own. I hope you spend your life chasing your dreams and not anyone else's. There is no one else like you. The deeper you can engrain that into your head, the better off you'll be.

I love you. I don't talk to you enough. I hope you always talk to me. I might be angry or hurt or disappointed, but I will always try to find a way to help you through it. I don't expect you to be perfect. Just be honest, no matter how ugly it is.

Honesty is ugly; deception is beautiful. Remember that and you will save yourself a lot of time in your relationships.

I love the way I look in the morning or with my hair in a bun on top of my head. I hate that I can't just accept myself, faults and all. I hope you ignore my insecurities and learn from them. I am wrong about myself, but I am not wrong about you. You are beautiful, my dear. All of you. You don't need makeup, fancy clothes, or fancy titles. Just you is enough. It really is. Find a partner in life who thinks that, too.

I believe when the time is right, I will fall in love again. I don't believe I am patient enough to wait for it. You may not be patient either, but you won't find love on your timeline. When it's meant to happen, it will happen at the exact right moment, and not a second too soon. You will hate it when your well-meaning friends tell you this, but they are right. Listen. Then go rule the world. You don't need a partner to rule the world. But if you choose to have one, he or she, depending on your preference, should bring out the best in you. If they don't, be done with them.

I love that I am fearless on some things. I hate that I am fearful on others. You are fearless, child. And you have been since the day you were born. Don't ever lose that.

I hope you never try to please everyone. You will fail because it is impossible to please

everyone. My sincere hope is that you try to please
no one. Do what you love. Be honest. Be one
hundred percent you. And let the chips fall where
they may. You cannot be responsible for other
people's emotions. Not even mine. Your life is yours.
Go live it.

   My final advice to you, dear daughter,
comes from the last part of William Cullen Bryant's
famous poem, "Thanaptosis." These words do not
live in my head but in my soul, and they created the
gumption that allowed me to walk out the door and
burn it all down.

> So live, that when thy summons
> comes to join
> The innumerable caravan, which
> moves
> To that mysterious realm, where
> each shall take
> His chamber in the silent halls of
> death,
> Thou go not, like the quarry-slave
> at night,
> Scourged to his dungeon, but,
> sustained and soothed
> By an unfaltering trust, approach
> thy grave,
> Like one who wraps the drapery of
> his couch
> About him, and lies down to
> pleasant dreams.

221

I was scared when you were born. Scared in a way that everyone should be—to die without ever having lived. But more so, I was scared that you would, too.

It is my hope that when the Reaper comes to wrap his arms around you, you will lie down to pleasant dreams, knowing that every moment you lived was, in fact, *lived*. And, as Frank Sinatra crooned, you did it your way.

So, regret nothing, daughter, unless it is because you have not lived or have not loved, especially yourself. This is my wish for you. Peace where it counts. In the depths of your soul.

What are you waiting for? Live the life we fought so hard for.

All my love,
Mom

The End

Made in the USA
Columbia, SC
18 September 2023